Servant Leadership in Business

Today's Practical Leadership Strategies to Inspire and Grow Your Team While Achieving Your Business Goals

By

Kenneth Hunter

entertainment purposes only. All effort has been executed to present accurate, up to date, and reliable, complete information. No warranties of any kind are declared or implied. Readers acknowledge that the author is not engaging in the rendering of legal, financial, medical or professional advice. The content within this book has been derived from various sources. Please consult a licensed professional before attempting any techniques outlined in this book.

By reading this document, the reader agrees that under no circumstances is the author responsible for any losses, direct or indirect, which are incurred as a result of the use of information contained within this document, including, but not limited to, — errors, omissions, or inaccuracies.

Table of Contents

Introduction

The perfect description of today's world is one where self-interest pre-occupies the business of leadership. Social, economic, political and even religious settings are meticulously designed to operate in some sort of a perpetual rat race. In such an environment, orderly and formal as it may look on the outside lies within it the void and dysfunctionality created by the absence of servant leadership.

The concept of servant leadership is alien and unorthodox in the fast-paced, self-centered 21st century we all live in. Heroism, unethical maneuvers, and immoral practices characterize behavioral patterns in society at the expense of the well-being and advancement of others.

Leadership is a responsibility which means the person occupying the office must have the capacity and ability to respond to the needs of others. There are different approaches leaders may assume. Some respond through autocracy, others through benevolent dictatorship, still some go down the laissez-faire way where everyone gets to share their opinions and do things in whichever way they like.

Which Leadership Stone are You Hewn From?

Leadership goes beyond the title. It involves taking on responsibility and nurturing others. With a little study, hard work, and humility, everyone can be an effective leader. That said, every person has a starting point and yours begins here.

Follow the link below and take the quiz to assess your baseline performance in servant leadership. For each question, answer as honestly as you can. Your response should reflect what you actually are, instead of what you think you should be. Good luck!

http://testyourleadership.site/

Servant leadership is different. It is a conscious decision by a leader to use their emergent authority guided by ethical and moral guardrails to serve others. As opposed to a leader-first approach, this style of leadership is people-first and people-centered. It turns conventional leadership on its head and adopts an inverted pyramid approach to business management.

Leaders have the capacity to make or break, to construct or deconstruct, to plant or uproot. Such phenomenal power requires a leadership style whose success can be measured in objective terms and not through ambiguous metrics. Servant leadership is one such style. Its success can be measured by how well and better those who are led become.

It is a compound form of leadership bringing together a cocktail of principles, practices, approaches, and behavioral patterns that culminate in an interconnected and inseparable framework fusing the qualities of servanthood into the concept of leadership.

To those grounded in mundane leadership perspectives, servant leadership may seem a lofty and mirage-like sensation whose ideals are unearthly and unattainable. For this reason, it is not unusual for servant leadership to be greeted with cynicism and suspicion.

Businesses exist to create value by solving specific societal problems. Servant leadership is inherently embedded in the value creation process. It focuses on the most important component of this process which is the human resource. There is no meaningful value that can be created if the human resource capacity is undermined or underprioritized. It is the engine of change that must kick on and chug along the train of transformation.

The question of how to create a super workforce has been the subject of strategies, plans of action and monitoring and evaluation approaches put in place by companies all over the world. Little do most of these organizations know that without servant leadership, any arrangement to bring the best in human resource is nothing more than a house of cards.

Servant leadership is the glue that holds everything together. It is a theory of leadership that is both emotionally satisfying and intellectually compelling. It is relevant and applicable to any workplace setting irrespective of their unique dynamism. It cuts through clutter, noise, mediocrity, and vagueness to shore up a style of leadership that is dependable and visionary.

The holistic nature of servant leadership demands that no one should be left behind. Leaders and followers are to forge forward through a mechanism that is service-oriented, focused on authenticity, morally courageous, and transformative. The result of this collaboration is a metamorphosed leader-follower structure that brings out the best in everyone.

The genesis of servant leadership is the desire to scale others up to become what they are capable of becoming. On the part of the leader, it entails positive use of power and influence to enhance their leadership roles. It purposely combines servanthood and leadership to create a servant-first leadership model.

In this unique follower-centered approach, the leader assumes the role of a steward. They view their followers as people who have been entrusted to them with the principal aim of elevating them to better versions of themselves.

According to Richard L. Daft and Robert H. Lengel, the hallmark of servant leaders is their dedication and deliberate choice to serve others. This principle is captured very well in some corporate organizations. Good examples are Starbucks, Balfour Beatty, Datron World Communication, Marriott International and many others as captured in the opening chapter of this book.

Servant leadership has been proved over time as a credible foundation for both personal and organizational excellence. Contextually, we live in an era where the need for servant leadership cannot be overemphasized. Destructive leadership in organizations manifested through high profile scandals continue to make headlines all over the world. The effects of such immoral and unethical leadership practices include demoralized workers, job tension, deviant behavior, emotional fatigue abuse of power, and so on. None of these makes a successful organization.

While traditional leadership models emphasize performance-oriented strategies, servant leadership goes beyond the profit and growth limitation. It changes mindsets impressed during the industrial revolution where people were merely viewed as units of production into a new mindset that considers human resource as emotional, relational, and ethical. This is the change that has been credited with turnarounds in organizations and transformative innovations in R&D departments.

Contemporary organizations are increasingly shifting their focus on value-based systems. Descriptive words such as transparency, accountability, customer service, compassion, honesty, and humility are appearing more often incorporate strategic plans, social media outreaches and in annual reports. However, unless such values are rooted in a solid servant leadership model, they can never influence product and service delivery at the organizational level.

Despite the confusion and dissatisfaction brought about by current leadership styles, there is hope both now and in the future. Any organization that is true to itself can begin the journey to complete transformation by embracing the principles and values of servant leadership. It has been done before and your organization can do it starting now.

The only prerequisite to servant leadership is the desire to serve which should then be followed by the desire to lead. However paradoxical it may seem; servant leadership is the anchor that can steady your organization and the sails that can positively tap into the winds of change to create a super business model that disrupts conventional corporate wisdom.

Read along! The chapters that follow will take you to the very heart of servant leadership, giving you practical steps and invaluable principles on how to roll out this form of leadership irrespective of the size of your organization. Let us dig right in! shall we?

Chapter 1: Understanding the Concept of Servant Leadership

As a leader, have you ever taken some time to talk to your followers about how they think of you as a leader? If you have, what did they say? If you have not, what do you think they would say? Would your followers describe you as a servant leader with how you are right now?

As aforementioned, not all people understand the concept of servant leadership. However, it is much easier for those who have a rare, yet strong, desire to serve other people. Think about how you feel about leadership now, do you want to climb all the way to the top in order to get fame, status, money, and power? Or do you want to help others and lift them up (along with your entire company) with you? If upon reflection, you realize that you are the latter, you would always feel compelled to serve first. This means that you have great potential to become a servant leader.

If you are the former but you are also

interested in the concept of becoming a servant leader, good for you! Just keep in mind that being a leader but having the heart of a servant is an invaluable asset. In fact, all leaders should try to adopt this kind of mentality, especially if they want to grow along with their people and with their organization as well.

A lot of people confuse the concept of leadership with that of dictatorship. But dictators bark out orders without considering the needs and wants of other people. On the other hand, servant leaders do the exact opposite. They work tirelessly with the aim of developing their people. They focus on how they can serve other people, especially their followers. To give you a better understanding of the concept of servant leadership, let's take a look at some examples:

1. **Allowing other people to see you serving those around you and encouraging them to follow suit**

    It is important for your clients, employees, and the other leaders in your organization to witness you in service. For instance, if your company started a donation drive for the benefit of a charity in your community, start by donating relevant items and encourage others to do the same.

2. However, do not just show your service for the sake of lifting yourself up

Make sure that everyone knows that you genuinely care. For instance, if you notice one of your employees struggling with his workload, approach him. Ask him the reason why he's struggling and if you can do anything to help out.

3. See your people as a valuable investment

Doing this makes it easier for you to serve them with all of your heart. For instance, you can spend time with your people, get to know them, and let them know that you are always there to help if they need you. Take a genuine interest in your people and, in doing this, you will see how your efforts will affect their job performance.

4. When it comes to serving others, do not restrict or limit your willingness

As a servant leader, no form of service is "beneath you." You should never think or feel that you are above manual labor. Most employees sense this attitude and it is very off-putting. For instance, if your company started a clean-up activity in your community, do not be afraid to join everyone else as they work together to clean up the neighborhood.

All successful servant leaders maintain a true servant's heart. While serving others, they also encourage their followers and the people around them to serve as well. Can you imagine how amazing your company will become if everyone starts thinking this way? How will this affect the overall experience of your clients and customers? The bottom line is that only good can come when you show your people how good it feels to serve first.

Defining servant leadership

When it comes to leadership, there is no "one-size-fits-all" definition. Any leader can succeed no matter what their personality is, their education level, their style or the theories they use to guide them. Basically, as long as you commit to being a leader by following your own preferred leadership style, you will find success. However, this does not mean that you are being the best leader you can be. Although you are doing a good job, there is always room for improvement. One way to improve your leadership style is to learn how to become a servant leader.

By definition, servant leadership is a set of practices as well as a philosophy which enriches your life as an individual and as a leader. Servant leadership helps build more productive organizations. Ultimately, it helps create a world that is more caring and just. If this definition invokes in your strong positive emotions, then you are definitely fit to become a servant leader.

Servant leadership is not a new concept at all. The term was coined by Robert Greenleaf in the year 1970 where he also said that "The servant leader is servant first." Unlike "traditional leaders" who tend to be more authoritarian, servant leaders do not work to gain or exercise their power over others within their companies. Rather, servant leaders:

- Think about the needs of their people first. They concentrate on fulfilling the most important needs of other people. They have a strong sense of responsibility and caring for those around them.

- Commit to helping their people improve in terms of their performance. They also help their people grow and develop in their area of expertise. Servant leaders consider the professional and personal development of other people as their priority. They also help build the professional skills and knowledge base of others.

- Insist that their company make positive

contributions to the community. While maintaining their focus, servant leaders also make sure that their community, region or nation improves with the help of their company.

In terms of different leader styles, servant leadership is a lot like participative leadership. This is a classic approach to leadership which has a positive long-term effect on the improvement of the organization and the society it is in. As a servant leader, genuinely caring for your employees encourages them to treat others the same way whether it be their colleagues, the clients of your company, and other people outside of the company as well.

Servant leadership promotes trust which, in turn, improves the credibility of your organization. It promotes a corporate culture that is positive in order to motivate the employees to perform better. This is because servant leaders pay more attention to their people while helping them improve.

According to the Theory of Servant Leadership, work must always give the employees opportunities to keep on learning so that they can grow professionally to accomplish their goals and be the best version of themselves. And when employees improve, the company they work in improves as well. So if you want to develop along with your colleagues and your people, you may want to commit to servant leadership.

A short history of servant leadership

Although the concept of servant leadership began about two thousand years ago, in this modern world, the movement known as servant leadership was introduced by Robert K. Greenleaf back in the year 1970 when he published his classic essay entitled, "The Servant Leader." In this essay, he coined the terms, "servant leadership" and "servant leader."

According to Greenleaf, the servant leader is always a servant first. This means that servant leaders have the heart of a servant which gives them an innate desire to serve others. This is one of the most fundamental characteristics of servant leaders. It is not just about being excessively willing to serve others. It is more about wanting to serve. It is about being able to identify and meet all of the needs of one's followers, colleagues, clients, and community.

The concept of servant leadership according to Greenleaf was inspired by the book written by Herman Hesse entitled, "Journey to the East." The book focuses on a group of people who traveled and their servant Leo. This man performed all of the menial chores of the group and he kept their spirits lifted with songs and his positive spirit.

Everything was going well until one day, Leo disappeared. When this happened, the travelers fell into chaos which they could not get out of. Because of Leo's disappearance, their journey came to an end. A few years after, one of the travelers met Leo once again. But now, he saw Leo revered as the head of the Order which sponsored their journey. Leo, the man whom they saw as their servant, was actually the noble head of the Order and he was truly a great leader.

In Greenleaf's essay, he said that this story clearly shows how a great leader is "seen as a servant first." Simple as this fact is, it is the key to being a great and successful leader. All the while, Leo was already the leader. But he started off as the servant of the group because deep inside, that was who he was. By nature, this man was a servant thus, he was bestowed with leadership. This honor was something assumed or given but which would also be taken away. Leo, the man, was a servant by nature and this could not be taken away from him.

Although servant leadership involves several characteristics, there is one which stands out in the essay written by Greenleaf and that is the desire to serve. Later on, we will be discussing the other important characteristics in detail as provided by Greenleaf since these are the ones which he considered important for servant leaders. These characteristics are listening, empathy, healing, awareness, persuasion, conceptualization, foresight, stewardship, commitment to the growth of people, and building community.

According to Greenleaf's description of servant leaders, they are those who initiate action, focus on goals, dream great dreams, communicate well, and those who can reorient themselves. Servant leaders are also highly situational, trusted, intuitive, creative, and dependable.

Apart from Greenleaf, scholars have also tried identifying some relevant characteristics of servant leaders with the purpose of testing and developing theories about the effects of servant leadership. For instance, Professor Robert Liden along with his colleagues came up with the dimensions of servant leadership which they utilized as part of their research. These dimensions were servanthood, emotional healing, conceptual skills, creating value for one's community, empowering, putting one's subordinates first, helping one's subordinates succeed and grow, relationships, and behaving ethically.

Also, the author Dirk van Dierendonck

performed a review of the scholarly literature in order to come up with the key characteristics of the behaviors of servant leaders namely empowering and developing others, authenticity, humility, interpersonal acceptance, stewardship, and providing direction.

When Greenleaf describes servant leadership, he describes it as a philosophy and not just a theory. But for those who want to take the other theories about servant leadership into consideration, you will discover that it has unique aspects compared with other leadership theories and these are:

- The moral aspect of servant leadership, not just in terms of the servant leader's personal integrity and morality but also with regard to how servant leaders encourage improved moral reasoning among his followers. Therefore, this tests the moral foundation of the organizational goals and visions of the servant leader.

- The focus which is on serving others for

the good of the company and for the good of the employees too. Also, it is about creating long-term relationships with one's followers while promoting their growth, improvement, and development for them to reach their full potential.

- The genuine concern for the success of everyone in the company from the employees to the stakeholders, the clients, and more even the ones who are least privileged.

- The self-reflection aspect which counters the hubris of leaders.

As aforementioned, the founder of modern servant leadership is Robert K. Greenleaf. The essay he wrote stemmed from his concerns over the qualities of centralized organizational structures being used as a management style in an attempt to run companies successfully. Part of this belief may have been formed back when Greenleaf worked at AT&T. This belief evolved further when he founded the Greenleaf Center for Servant Leadership back in the year 1964.

After he took an early retirement, Greenleaf became a corporate consultant while he promoted his work. Since his death, the center he founded has maintained his life's mission to promote the awareness of servant leadership for the improvement of corporate cultures.

Greenleaf felt suspicious about those who chose to lead first. He believed that they had a need to gain power in their organizations just to acquire all of the material possessions they wanted. But for Greenleaf, he saw more potential in the idea of serving others first wherein the servant leader should make sure that the highest priority needs of his people are served.

Now, more and more people are becoming interested in the concept of servant leadership. The great thing about servant leadership is that it has a lot of useful concepts which you can apply to businesses in order for them to operate more efficiently and effectively.

The advantages and disadvantages of servant leadership

Servant leadership has the potential to enrich an individual's life, build more effective organizations, and it creates a better world. This is because servant leaders focus on the well-being and growth of their people and of the communities to which these leaders belong. Although Robert Greenleaf pioneered the philosophy of servant leadership back in the 1960s and 1970s, it has become more relevant today. This is because organizations are mostly defined by their people. When empowering your people so that they can reach their potential, you are actually giving yourself and your company an edge over the competition.

When you apply servant leadership to businesses, it fosters a corporate culture of collaboration, respect, and, ultimately, success. But for you to be able to experience all of these advantages, you must carefully think about your relationship with your people and with your organization. Servant leadership is so effective because it focuses on people. This is why leaders all over the world are starting to adopt this style of leadership. Let's take a look at the most significant advantages of servant leadership you may expect:

⚬ **It empowers people**

Remember that servant leaders focus on their people. When employees feel that their leaders genuinely care for them and want to see them succeed, this empowers them. Because of this, they start working with a more positive and motivated attitude compared to those who feel like they are nothing but a cog in a big corporate machine.

For servant leaders, behavior is not just about getting things done, it is about how they get things done. At the end of the day, this behavior becomes transformative for the employees. Because of how you treat them, speak to them, and serve them, they feel empowered enough to do their best. Also, they do not feel any hesitation to offer their own suggestions and contributions. In turn, they start treating each other as well as the company's clients and customers with the same type of care and service. Also, when you make your employees feel appreciated, this leads to improved innovation, production, and retention.

⏹ It makes leaders stronger

Although some people do not see why leaders must serve their people, doing this actually makes you a stronger leader. Since you engage and inspire your employees through servant leadership, doing this helps you out as well. As a servant leader, people will not be afraid to communicate with you openly, especially about the things you need to know.

Also, there is a higher likelihood that your people will follow you no matter how bold or how out-of-the-box your vision is. Even if you do not remind them, your people will have the initiative to do the things they need to do. Your people will start performing better and they will start watching out for you to protect you from any negativity and nefarious deeds. And as you experience all of these changes, it will encourage you further to become a more effective servant leader. Soon, you can start encouraging others to do the same for their own good and for the good of the company.

▢ It propels organizations

Michael Bush, the CEO of Great Place to Work describes what servant leaders can potentially achieve for their companies. When leaders give up their traditional autocratic ways, employees within the organization feel more passionate about their work. They tend to be more innovative, collaborative, and they work harder too. All of these behaviors help propel organizations.

When you see how passionately your people work, this will make you feel more passionate as well. Then you can start working together for the benefit of your own company. Basically, servant leadership can be a powerful force which drives positive change and the best part about it is that being a servant leader is not a difficult thing!

⦾ It helps leaders teach others to lead themselves

When it comes to servant leadership, service is its primary focus. This means that you may have to set aside your own desires and wishes in order to listen and work with those under your leadership. As you help your people, they start learning how to help themselves too. Soon, they will start learning how to be efficient servant leaders themselves.

Part of servant leadership is enabling others to lead. You have to eliminate the authoritarian atmosphere. Rather, you listen to your people and facilitate a collaborative approach to running your organization. And when all of your employees have gotten used to this culture, you will notice your company running more smoothly as your employees work passionately towards a single goal.

⬚ It provides a sense of responsibility

Servant leadership gives everyone a sense of responsibility. It enables those you are leading to share the responsibility and feel a sense of ownership for their own work. This, in turn, increases their dedication along with their sense of pride when they are able to accomplish tasks successfully. As this is happening, you should see the productivity of your organization improve.

Since the servant leader shows trust, respect, and genuine concern for his employees, this encourages them to do the same. As the positive atmosphere in the workplace continues, employees are motivated, encouraged, and inspired to support each other and come together for their own benefit and for the benefit of the company.

⬚ It allows for diversity

Within any kind of company or organization, there are different types of people with different traits, talents, personalities, and different ways of working too. As a servant leader, you would recognize all of these differences and accept your people for who they are.

Servant leaders recognize that the diversity of their people is crucial to the success of their company. Diversity is one thing that authoritarian leaders leave little room for. They want everyone to "be the same" because it is easier for them to manage. However, that can be extremely frustrating for a lot of employees. But thanks to the flexibility of servant leadership, diversity is not seen as an issue. Instead, it is seen as something which will improve the effectiveness of the organization.

⬜ It involves and benefits everyone

Basically, servant leadership does not just benefit the leader. Since servant leadership encourages leaders to form stronger, more meaningful relationships with their people, this makes everyone part of it. As a servant leader, you do not just focus on yourself or on specific employees. You serve everyone, no matter how insignificant they might seem. You encourage everyone to be engaged with each other. You also promote the sense of community within the organization. Moreover, when your people see that you are always willing to serve others around you, they will learn to do the same. Thus, being a servant leader actually benefits everyone.

These are the most important advantages of servant leadership; however, there are a lot more. But just like anything else in this world, servant leadership is not perfect. This means that it also comes with a couple of disadvantages you should know about, such as:

- One of the biggest disadvantages of servant leadership is that it may take some time for you to start this venture. In order for you to become a successful servant leader, you need to make a change both in your mentality and attitude. When you start on this journey, easy as it is for you to do, you cannot really set a "deadline" for it.

- Another disadvantage is that a lot of people might not be willing to adopt the leadership style along with you. It would be very difficult to be the only one in your organization willing to become a servant leader.

- Some say that another disadvantage is that employees might not see you as their leader when you are in the business of serving them. Although some employees might appreciate their leader as a servant, others might not be on board with it.

- Then there may also be some confusion, especially in terms of leadership goals. Your people might think that you do not really know how to lead them which is why you serve them instead.

- Also, some people might not see

servant leadership as a match for their type of business.

These are the most common disadvantages of servant leadership. Of course, this does not mean that they outweigh the advantages. Later on, we will be talking more about the challenges faced by servant leaders, how to overcome these challenges and apply the concept to the modern business world. For now, let's take a look at why servant leadership is good for organizations.

Why is servant leadership good for organizations?

Most of the time, people do not believe in something until they have seen, heard, or read proof about it. There is nothing wrong with this kind of thinking, of course. In fact, in this modern world that is filled with hoaxes and false information, it is understandable why people want to be convinced further before they believe in such things. The good news about servant leadership is that it is not just some philosophy thought up by one person. It has been around for a long time now and Robert Greenleaf merely brought the concept in all its entirety into the modern world because he believed in it so much.

There has been a lot of research and studies done on servant leadership. All of them show that in terms of how it positively impacts the leader, the people, and the organization, nothing beats servant leadership. If you are still not convinced, here are some studies and reasons for you to think about:

- ⬜ **High organizational effectiveness**

  A man named Dr. Robert Liden who is a Professor of Management at the University of Illinois had conducted several studies about how servant leadership builds collaboration and strong teams (Liden, 2019). These studies have shown how servant leadership helps improve the performance of businesses.

- ⬜ **Employee helpfulness and**

creativity

According to a study, the employees of effective servant leaders display more helpfulness and creativity compared to those who have leaders who do not practice servant leadership (Bier & O'Reilly, 2015).

⬜ **Employees feeling more satisfied with their jobs**

A study conducted at a 5-hospital system showed that the nurses who worked with nurse managers with a high servant leadership orientation felt more satisfied with their jobs (Jenkins & Stewart, 2010).

⬜ **Confidence and high performance**

Another study was conducted this time in 5 different banks (Hu & Liden, 2011). The study showed that servant leaders help make their people more confident by affirming their strengths, the team's potential, and providing them with development support.

▢ Higher employee engagement

In 2008, the Cleveland Clinic study showed that servant leadership helped increase the engagement of employees along with the overall satisfaction of the patients (Partnchak, 2016).

▢ Improved business

Another study performed at the University of Illinois was conducted about the Jason's Deli restaurants in the US. According to this study, bosses who act as servants makes for improved business. They saw improvements in employee job performance, customer service, and the retention of employees (When bosses 'serve' their employees, everything improves, 2015).

▢ Turns businesses around

The global restaurant chain known as Popeye's Louisiana Kitchen experienced an incredible business turnaround as documented in the latest book for their CEO entitled, "Dare to Serve." In this book, Cheryl Bachelder described how their company went from being at the edge of disaster to one which experienced a huge growth all because their leaders decided to adapt servant leadership (Bachelder, 2019).

☐ **Outperforming the competition**

Finally, there was a group of researchers who made a comparison regarding the Good to Great companies which Jim Collins made famous. These companies have applied the principles of servant leadership. According to this research, during the years when they conducted the study, the stocks of these companies averaged a more than 10% portfolio return pre-taxes (Linchtenwalner, n.d.).

Apart from these studies, you will also see a lot of proof just by doing your own research about the companies which exist today. Here are some examples of well-known companies which are benefitting from servant leadership:

Balfour Beatty

The CEO of this construction company, Eric

Stenman has a firm belief in servant leadership. He believes in this philosophy so much that he applies it to his own company. Stenman always focuses on the professional and personal success of everyone in his company.

Datron World Communication

In the year 2004, the head of this company, Art Barter, purchased it for $10 million and in 5 years, he turned it into a company worth $200 million. He did this by applying the servant leadership model to the company.

Marriott International

The founder of this company, Bill Marriott has always focused on a corporate culture of service which he applies to his organization as well as to his clients. He emphasizes "the spirit to serve" which, he believes is what is moving his organization to success.

Nordstrom

This famous department store has a huge loyal fan base because they place a lot of focus on their customers. Unbeknownst to most people, this company has an organizational model known as the "inverted pyramid" wherein they place the floor and sales staff at the highest priority level while the directors and the executive team are at the bottom level. The Nordstrom brothers had also started at the lowest level and they worked hard to reach the top. So their decision to use this organizational model is not surprising at all.

Starbucks

Although small coffee shop owners see this company as the bane of their existence, the service they provide to their employees is exceptional. Aside from giving non-standard benefits to its employees, the company has also started helping their employees pay for their college tuition. Howard Schultz, the CEO of the company believes in linking the value of their shareholders to the value of their employees.

The Container Store

Kip Tindell, the CEO of this company has

frequently talked about how he does not believe in focusing on maximizing returns to their shareholders. Instead, he prioritizes his employees as he believes that a strong organizational community is crucial to the success of the business.

Chapter 2: The 10 Characteristics of Servant Leadership

Servant leaders are always "servants first" which means that they prioritize the needs of other people, especially their followers before they consider their own needs. As a servant leader, you acknowledge the perspective of other people, provide them with genuine support, make them part of the decision-making process whenever appropriate, and create a sense of community within the team. In doing this, you will see an improvement in terms of engagement, trust, and the strength of your relationship with your followers and with the stakeholders of the company.

Servant leadership is considered as a technique, a style, and behaving in such a way which you adopt for a long time. Basically, you would focus more on the needs of other people as you lead them to success. To do this, you may have to make a couple of changes to how you lead your people now. Even if you are not a leader, you can learn how to become a servant leader and we will be discussing this later on.

If one of your professional and personal goals is to become a servant leader, then you must be aware of the 10 characteristics to have. As described by Larry Spears, the former president of the Greenleaf Center for Servant Leadership, these 10 characteristics will help you out in the long-run. Learning and practicing these characteristics enables you to prioritize the needs of other people over your own. While these characteristics are fairly basic, there are some skills you have to learn to excel in each of them. Before discussing these characteristics in detail, let's have a quick rundown of them:

⍰ **Listening**

If you learn how to listen deeply, intently, and genuinely to your people, you will be able to serve them more effectively. Listening is not just about hearing what they are saying. You also have to understand the message they are trying to convey by noticing their gestures and body language. As you listen to others, make sure that you are giving them your full attention and you do not interrupt them as they are speaking. Only when they are done talking would it be appropriate to respond or give feedback.

☐ Empathy

Servant leaders always strive to comprehend the perspectives and intentions of other people. To be a more empathic leader, you must temporarily set aside your own viewpoint, value the perspectives of others, and approach each situation openly.

☐ Healing

This is related to the emotional "wholeness" and the health of other people which means that you have to give them your support both mentally and physically. To do this, you must make sure that everyone has the required resources, support, and knowledge needed to perform their jobs well. Also, you must make sure that your employees work in a healthy environment. After this, you can take the necessary steps to make your people feel happier and more engaged overall.

⁂ **Awareness**

To become a good servant leader, you must learn more about yourself first. Reflect profoundly on your behaviors and your emotions. Understand your advantages and disadvantages. Then think about how these impact those surrounding you and how these align with your own values. You must also learn how to keep your emotions in check and think about how your actions affect those around you.

⁂ **Persuasion**

Instead of using their authority, servant leaders use persuasion. This is a more effective way to encourage others to take action. As a servant leader, you must learn the art of persuasion in order to build credibility which, in turn, makes it easier for your people to listen to you and follow you.

☐ **Conceptualization**

This characteristic enables you to see the "bigger picture." As a leader, you should be able to conceptualize in order to develop an organizational strategy that is robust, effective, and realistic. After conceptualizing, you must also be able to create vision and mission statements which contain clear explanations of the roles your people will play in the long-term objectives of your organization.

☐ **Foresight**

This characteristic enables you to predict the likeliest outcome by learning from your experiences in the past, observing the current situation, and by understanding what happens because of the decisions you have made. It isalso important for you to trust in your own intuition as part of this characteristic.

☐ **Stewardship**

This   is   all   about   you   taking

responsibility for all of the actions as well as the overall performance of your people. You should learn to be accountable for all of the roles your people play in the organization.

☐ **Commitment to the growth of people**

As a servant leader, you must commit yourself to the professional and personal development of your people. You must look for strategies and training to help your people develop until they reach their full potential.

☐ **Building community**

Finally, you must also be able to build a sense of community within your whole organization. To do this, you must allow them to interact with one another freely, both in the business setting and outside of the workplace too.

Listening

All types of leaders must have superior decision-making and communicating skills. But as a servant leader, you must also have superior listening skills. You should have the ability to listen genuinely to your people both as individuals and as groups or teams. This is important to help you determine their wills or desires. Aside from listening to others, you must also learn how to listen to your own self to find out what motivates you.

Listening is the first characteristic of servant leadership. Although communication and decision-making skills are highly valued, servant leaders must also have a profound commitment to listen intently and genuinely to other people. Servant leaders must always receptively listen to what their people are saying as well as to the unsaid things. This skill also involves thoughtful reflection as both important to the well-being and growth of any servant leader.

In this modern world, we are all driven by a desire to communicate and connect with others. However, because of this desire, we often get lost in the sheer amount of information coming in thus, we end up taking our listening skills for granted. Whether you are communicating with your people online or in person, listening remains to be the fundamental building block of communication as well as the key to creating strong and deep relationships.

Think about it, when you want your superior to hear what you have to say, how would you convey your message? Whether you speak to your own boss directly with a long speech you have prepared, or you send him a succinct email which contains all of your great ideas, do you think your boss will get your message if he does not know how to listen well? Chances are, he will not.

Let's have an example to illustrate the value of this characteristic. For instance, one of your employees wants to share an idea about how to boost the morale of everyone at the office. Most leaders would probably hear out this employee without really listening to him or taking him seriously. In the end, change does not happen because the leaders did not really listen to what the employee had to say.

But as a servant leader, when someone approaches you with such an idea (and if you are an effective servant leader, your people will not hesitate to communicate openly with you), you would invite this employee into your office to listen to what he has to say. Instead of brushing the idea or suggestion off, you would start a conversation about it.

You ask your employee about his idea, the situation which brought this idea on, what your employee thinks should change, and you might even invite other employees in to share the discussion with you. All the while, you are also observing your employee's body language, his gestures, the tone of his voice, and everything else that he does not express verbally.

In the first scenario, change does not happen within the workplace. Therefore, the employees work just as they always did.

And the employee who wanted his voice to be heard probably feels bad about being overlooked or brushed off by his superiors. But in the second scenario, the servant leader genuinely listened to his employee. He started a discussion, involved other people, and made a change which, in turn, helped boost the morale and productivity of the employees as a whole.

Simple as this example may seem, it is a very common situation in the modern workplace. More often than not, leaders do not have the time or interest to listen to their people. Sadly, this culture has become so common that employees do not even expect to be heard at all. So, no matter how incredible one's ideas or insights are, these are not brought into the light all because the people on top do not listen.

But as a servant leader, you should see the importance of listening. This characteristic allows you to become more knowledgeable about yourself, the people around you, and your organization too. The calling of servant leaders to serve depends on how well they listen and how well they are able to perceive the needs of those around them. So if you plan to become a servant leader, it is time to start working on your listening skills.

Empathy

By definition, empathy is a person's ability to comprehend and to share what other people feel. Empathy can be a response to negative or positive emotions. More often than not, empathy is communicated without words. In fact, you might have a better understanding of this characteristic when it is shown to you by other people. Empathy is another characteristic of servant leaders. As a servant leader, one of the ways you can show empathy towards your people is to realize that each individual is unique.

Traditional leaders tend to compare their employees and often, they end up thinking why one employee cannot be like another. Although some employees are not really "good" at their jobs, this does not mean that they are not good at anything. However, most leaders only see what they want to see. So no matter how hard their employees work, no matter how much they contribute to the team or to the organization, just because they do not excel in their job, leaders tend to overlook them.

But for servant leaders who have this characteristic, they do not allow themselves to focus on theoretical grandiosity as this makes them blind to trench reality. As a servant leader, you must have empathy for each and every one of your people in order to see them for who they really are and accept them for it. Then, you must model this characteristic with the other leaders in your organization in order for them to learn and acquire the same characteristic so they can feel and show empathy towards everyone else in the organization.

One incredible example of an empathic servant leader is Satya Nadella, the CEO of the Microsoft Corporation. Since Nadella became the CEO of the company, he has made a dramatic improvement in terms of reviving the relevance and reputation of the

Microsoft Corporation. He did this by emphasizing collaboration as well as a "learn-it-all culture" instead of the "know-it-all culture" which they have been practicing for the longest time.

Nadella has always demonstrated ontological humility. When he made a huge mistake at a conference for women engineers, he was met with criticism. But his reaction was to own up to this mistake and admit the biases which he did not realize at that time. Because of this, his credibility became stronger. Nadella has also demonstrated empathy regularly as he recognizes the perspectives of the company's employees and his co-leaders as important and real to them. Also, he makes sure to give these perspectives the same level of attention and respect as they do.

Servant leaders must also realize that everyone has their own strengths and weaknesses. As an empathic leader, you would help develop the strengths of your people continuously. However, you will not sit idly by as you witness the weaknesses of your people either. Instead, you would approach your people about these weaknesses, talk to them about it, and help them figure out how to turn their weaknesses into strengths. Empathic leaders help open the doors to the self-actualization, self-fulfillment, and self-awareness of those around them.

Empathy also involves having a genuine concern for other people. Taking a moment to ask someone "How are you?" and coupling this with listening and empathy will help you become more engaged with your employees. Through these characteristics (and the others which we will be discussing), you will be able to initiate conversations and build profound, meaningful relationships with your people.

Servant leaders are able to empathize with individuals as well as with groups. Although this characteristic might feel crippling to some people, servant leaders do not allow their empathy to control them. Instead, they use empathy to make better decisions, especially about the people around them. Basically, having this characteristic allows you to look past the issues on the surface in order to find out the reality of the situation.

Healing

All people (including leaders) are in one state of brokenness or another. No matter how successful one might seem, there is always something which does not work quite right. As a servant leader, you must be able to recognize this. Also, you must not ignore this reality then revert to punishing an individual when his brokenness becomes "inconvenient" for his work. In other words, servant leaders have the characteristic of healing which enables them to find ways to mend these broken people.

The ability to heal people and relationships is a very powerful force for integration and transformation. Therefore, having this characteristic is one of the most relevant strengths of servant leaders. As a leader, you must recognize your own brokenness as well as the brokenness of those around you. But you do not stop there. You also see this brokenness and imperfection as something to work on, something to make better.

Because of the potential of healing to make people's lives better, this is perhaps the most powerful characteristic of servant leadership. And the great thing about healing is that there are so many ways to do it. For instance, an organization can focus on the physical wellness of its employees. An organization can also do other things such as have programs which develop the emotional intelligence of the employees, provide them with "restorative time" to promote inner development, and so on. But for an organization to build this kind of culture, its leaders should personally have a desire to seek wholeness.

Any servant leader can become a healing influence. To do this, you must have a good healing vocabulary because words are a very powerful healing force. But beyond your words, your actions hold even more power. For instance, servant leaders must never have favorites. They must place value in the scope of humanity which comprises their entire organization. Now try to think about how you lead your people. Do you only value the ideas or work of specific employees? Do you only focus on your company's "best workers" or do you focus on and try to improve everyone?

In terms of business, the healing characteristic is not as easy to verbalize. But if you truly want to become a servant leader, you must consciously choose "wholeness" in order to become a healer. Start by choosing your own personal wholeness. Then start learning and speaking healing words. After this, you can purposefully facilitate wholeness for individuals and for your whole organization. As time goes by, you will notice the results and the positive impact of your actions as a servant leader.

Once in a while, you will encounter people in your organization who have "broken spirits" and who have been suffering from different kinds of emotional pain. This is an unavoidable aspect of being human. As a servant leader, you must recognize these people as see this as your chance to make them whole. This is one important way of serving your people. Therefore, you must see healing as a service and not as a "chore" which you "must do" for the sake of the company.

Of course, healing in business does not mean that you should try to heal any medical conditions of your people. Such conditions cannot be healed merely through your actions. But if one of your people is experiencing such ailments of diseases, you can help them deal with their situation better by showing genuine concern and by offering help whenever they need it. Healing as a characteristic of servant leadership means that you take responsibility for your people's welfare. As you see members of your team who do not perform as well as the others because they are broken, you help them heal to get them "back on track."

Awareness

According to Robert Greenleaf, awareness is a critical characteristic of servant leaders. Having awareness does not mean that you give solace. Instead, it is more about being an awakener and a "disturber." Efficient servant leaders are always reasonably disturbed and sharply aware. They do not seek solace because they have their own inner peace.

From the viewpoint of Greenleaf, the main purpose of this characteristic is for the servant leader to meet the needs of other people and to persuade them toward a "common good." This journey starts with self-awareness and you can only follow this journey by answering very basic questions about yourself successfully. When you do this, you become more aware of yourself. In turn, you start becoming more aware of other people and their needs.

Just like the other characteristics of servant leaders, awareness of oneself and of others is not one-dimensional. When you learn to be aware of issues, problems, and the like, you do not just move on. Rather, you should engage the people you lead actively while applying the other characteristics of servant leadership in order to develop holistically. Unfortunately, this is not the easiest thing to do, especially for busy leaders. But when you think about it, busy leaders are not really servant leaders. So you must find a way to incorporate awareness into your life by trying to make yourself less busy. This way, you can also focus on the more important things.

Typically, leaders are not aware of what their people are doing, thinking or feeling. For instance, try to think about a leader or a superior you had in the past. At any point, did you ever feel like he was aware of your actions, thoughts or feelings? If you had a "traditional" type of leader, then the answer to this question is probably "no." Sadly though, this is very common among leaders. On the other hand, servant leaders make it a point to be aware of both the obvious and subtle things going on in their lives and in the lives of the people around them.

Remember what Greenleaf said about servant leaders being "servants first." So after you become aware of what is happening around you, it is time to act appropriately. There is no point in wishing that issues, problems or conflicts will resolve themselves after some time. Generally, awareness of oneself and of others makes servant leaders stronger. Being aware will help you understand the issues which involve values, power, and ethics. As you become more aware, you learn how to view situations from a perspective that is more holistic and more integrated too.

It would take some time for you to practice self-awareness and awareness of others. Depending on what role you play in your organization, you may or may not have the luxury of time. Even if you are faced with such a situation, do not give up! If you have become aware of how busy you actually are, communicate the situation to the right people within your organization. Invite, encourage, and influence them to adapt self-awareness too. In doing this, you will build a complementary environment which contextualizes awareness proactively for the good of everyone.

As described by Tjan, Harrington, and Hsieh (2012), in terms of leadership effectiveness, self-awareness is the characteristic which has an edge over all the others. When they interviewed more than 100 leaders, they found out that leadership does not come from specific characteristics of traits which have been endowed. Rather, it comes from being aware of oneself, knowing your own strengths and weaknesses, understanding your own experiences, and how all of these develop your abilities. Only after you become fully aware of yourself will you be able to serve other people by extending your awareness to them too.

Persuasion

When it comes to persuasion, some people have a somewhat negative connotation with this term. This is mainly because persuasive people are seen as pushing too fast, too hard or pushing without sufficient intellect or data. Whenever someone encounters such a person, it can be extremely frustrating. However, this is not being "persuasive" at all, just "pushy."

So what is persuasion in the context of servant leadership?

Most people have experienced working with a leader who is overbearing. A lot of employees can also relate to leaders who enjoy picking favorites, playing office politics, and utilizing manipulation just to get the work done. There are plenty of terms to use for these kinds of behaviors and actions none of which is persuasion. As a matter of fact, you might even go as far as calling this "coercion" which is when someone in power persuades their subordinates to do a specific job or task through threats or force. Of course, this is far from what servant leaders do.

Basically, persuasion comes in many different forms but they all have the same result. Done properly, persuasion results in a willing partnership which is designed to achieve a shared goal or vision. The key here is "willingness" which means that both parties, in this case, the leader and the follower, agree to do everything that is needed in order to achieve the outcome they desire. This means that as a servant leader, you do not have to threaten your people just to get the job done. Rather, you must encourage your people and facilitate pathways which lead to co-discovery so that you can reach your goals together.

Often, busy leaders create an environment where their employees feel like objectified commodities with no humanity. They focus on profit, prestige, and power. For them, "unethical employees" must be terminated. These refer to employees who do not meet the company's standards, those who break the rules, and so on. But for the employees who are not meeting the expectations of the company, these bosses try pushing them forward first before they are terminated.

Most of the time, the issue is systemic meaning that there is not enough training, there are unclear expectations, and so on. As a servant leader, you would first seek to understand your people and the situation before you act and not the other way around. When you find a problem, you use your powers of persuasion to convince your people to act appropriately. You have a conversation with the employee, find out what is wrong, and try to come up with a solution together.

Take, for instance, a leader in a sales business. If the servant leader notices that one of his employees is not meeting the required quota, he will not terminate this employee right away. Instead, he will first communicate with his employee. He may find out that the employee is dealing with a personal problem thus, he is not motivated. What does the servant leader do?

He uses persuasion to open the eyes and

mind of his employee. He talks about the benefits of his business and how performing better will help improve his personal life as well. If the employee works hard and improves his performance, he will be able to move up the corporate ladder. More opportunities will open up for him and he will be able to provide for his family more. Upon knowing this, the employee realizes that his leader does not just see him as "just another employee."

Because of this, he feels more motivated to try harder, work harder, and improve his performance for his own good and for the good of the company. Of course, persuasion must be done right, especially if you want to make a good impact on your people instead of appearing too pushy or too forceful.

Conceptualization

According to Greenleaf, conceptualization refers to a person's ability to create a concept that is future-oriented in order to come up with a vision and mission. This, in turn, enables the leader and his people to find purpose in their work.

Conceptualization does not just happen. Servant leaders must encourage ownership in order to shape a vision. The best way to do this is by building long-term relationships with others. Effective servant leaders do not use other people in order to achieve their personal goals. Instead, they help others develop in order to equip them with the skills they need to achieve the goals of the organization. Therefore, servant leaders must clarify both the informal and formal expectations early on.

As a servant leader, you must be able to conceptualize crises which are an inevitable part of any organization. So while you are building relationships, you must come up with a process by which you will deal with any unfulfilled expectations. That way, if such situations arise, you are prepared for them and you know how to approach them.

As a leader, do you often try to dream about or conceptualize your organization's future? If you do this a lot, do you keep these dreams a secret or do you share them with others? Or are you the kind of person who "dreams out loud" along with everyone else while allowing other people to come up with their own conceptualizations? Servant leaders are the type of people who share their dreams and communicate them with others as a way to come up with a collective narrative. In this type of environment, there is a very small likelihood of hearing negative things like "I hate working here" and others.

If you want to be a true servant leader, you must learn big picture thinking. This helps inspire your people to think past their daily routine and beyond any issues they are dealing with right now. While traditional leaders only focus on immediate or short-term goals, servant leaders go beyond this.

They think of what their organization must do in order to get everything done, not just the present issue or situation. For instance, servant leaders would always look for tools, resources, and training which they know will help their people in the future.

As part of the conceptualization characteristic, servant leaders also want to nurture their own abilities so they can think of bigger things. If you want to become a servant leader you must learn how to use a conceptualizing perspective each time you are dealing with any present issues in your organization. This is one characteristic which requires practice and discipline if you want to master it and make it a part of yourself.

More often than not, traditional leaders focus too much on achieving immediate operational goals. Conversely, servant leaders must learn how to stretch their way of thinking in order to incorporate conceptualization. By nature, this characteristic is an important role for boards of directors or trustees. Even if you do not hold a position this high in your organization, you must learn to be conceptual in your orientation. Of course, you should not ignore the daily operational needs either. Basically, as a servant leader, you must find the right balance between the day-to-day approach and conceptual thinking.

The best way to gain this characteristic is by learning how to become a visionary. Instead of feeling content with how you are now and what your organization is at, think about how you can improve yourself, your people, and your entire organization. Since you have an important and unique role as a leader, you must think beyond the perspectives of your people. That way, you can share your ideas with them and, in turn, they also learn how to dream, conceptualize, and look at the bigger picture.

Foresight

Nowadays, not a lot of people use the term "foresight." This is probably because of the convenience provided by gadgets, devices, and other modern inventions. Because searching for knowledge and answers has become so easy, people are not as disciplined when it comes to analyzing how their actions today impact the outcomes of tomorrow. But according to Greenleaf, maintaining the characteristic known as foresight is important for servant leaders.

Foresight is a key characteristic which allows you as a servant leader to fully understand the lessons from your past, the realities of your present, and the most likely effects of the decisions you make to your future. Just like all the other characteristics of servant leadership, it is entirely possible for you to learn foresight.

As a servant leader, you must base your decisions on the past, the present, and the future. For instance, you need to hire an employee who will play a key role in the company. Of course, this process involves interviews, testing, and other procedures as per your company's hiring policies. Before you make your final decision, think about those who have held that same position in the past. What characteristics did that employee have? Did you experience any problems with that employee which you want to avoid with the person you plan to hire?

Then think about your present situation. Why do you need to hire this person? What role will the employee play? What qualifications or characteristics do you need from the person you should hire? Finally, think about the future. Do you plan to assign future projects to this employee? Do you need the employee for an expansion or for other similar endeavors? These are just some examples of questions you should ask yourself when you need to hire someone new for your organization.

Basically, it illustrates how you can apply foresight as a servant leader. As you can see, foresight involves thinking about past, present, and future situations and ideas before you make your decision. As a servant leader, you would consciously surround yourself with individuals who have different perspectives as you. This allows you to analyze all of the unplanned consequences of certain decisions.

Part of having foresight is being intuitive. The fact is both foresight and intuition flow from each other perpetually. The more you practice foresight, the more your decision-making skills become intuitive. And the more you depend on your intuition, the more you are able to practice foresight as a way to validate the decisions you make. You cannot rely on just one of them.

For instance, when you only depend on your intuition, this causes you to ignore validated feedback. It is like saying "I feel like this person is a good fit for the company so I should hire him right now." On the other hand, when you only depend on foresight, this may cause paralysis. It is like saying, "Although these people seem qualified, we also believed that the one we hired last time was qualified too but it did not work out. So there is no way I will make the final decision on who to hire." Essentially, your intuition comes from your own experiences and it is developed further through foresight.

In this modern world, servant leaders must have the ability to carefully analyze situations and people. Without doing this, they will not be able to make wise or ethical decisions. Refusing or failing to foresee things can be considered as a type of ethical failure. Think of it this way: when you make an ethical compromise today, this may result in a failure to take the appropriate actions at a time when you had the freedom to act or to make the right decision. If you do not think beyond the present, you are unable to make a good decision for the future. It is as simple as that.

Stewardship

By definition, a steward is a person who takes charge of something and makes sure to keep it in good condition for the benefit of others. Servant leaders who possess this characteristic feel more motivated when they think of the greater good rather than when they think of personal rewards or achievements. As a servant leader, you would take actions or make decisions using a "steward's mentality."

Greenleaf had a perception of all organizations and institutions wherein all employees from the lowest ranking to the highest ranking ones all play important roles in terms of holding their organizations as stewards for their community or society. Just like stewardship, servant leadership primarily assumes a dedication to serving others in order to meet their needs. This type of leadership also highlights other positive characteristics instead of focusing on control.

As a servant leader, you should see yourself as a steward. One who holds your people and your organization. You take care of your people as well as your organization so as not to break the trust of the people who placed you in that position. Stewardship is another valuable characteristic of servant leader, but it is not as common as the others. As a matter of fact, some people might not even know what it means and what it entails.

If as a leader, you discover that your people and the other leaders in your organization are unfamiliar with this concept, it is time to introduce it to them. This encourages you and all the other members of your organization to act in the best interest of each other and of the team. You can even use persuasion to convince your people why stewardship is in everybody's best interest.

Let's take a look at an example of this characteristic to help you understand it better. If you have been recently hired to be the leader of a group of people, this means that the people who hired you have entrusted this team to you. Therefore, as a servant leader, you help these people grow, develop, and learn how to be the best versions of themselves. This is how you maintain and nurture the team entrusted in your care. In the end, your people or the members of your team become beneficial to your employers, to the organization, to you, and to themselves. This means that everyone benefits from your service to them!

Stewardship emphasizes the best aspects of servant leadership. By practicing it, you are able to achieve your objectives and the objectives of your organization by properly managing the appropriate resources for the growth and development of your people. As a steward, you must also possess characteristics such as responsibility, altruism, and a respect for authority figures. Both as a servant leader and as a steward, you will be able to lead your organization well in order to achieve all of the goals and desires of the stakeholders. Here, your leadership goal is to fulfill your mission and create a sustainable organization.

Commitment to the growth of people

For this characteristic, servant leaders recognize that the most valuable resource they have is their people. Therefore, servant leaders must commit themselves to the growth, development, and well-being of their people. This is why servant leaders prioritize the needs of their people over their own. In order to allow your people to grow, give them opportunities for promotions, training, and other types of activities which promote professional growth. Provide these to your people instead of just thinking of yourself. As a servant leader, you do not focus too much in your own place or position neither would you keep all of the best opportunities secret just so only you can take them.

Servant leaders must believe in the intrinsic value of people. Even though they might not seem too "valuable" on the outside because they do not excel in their job, they still have worth. This is why servant leaders must commit to the growth of each person in their organization. This way, they can help their people improve and reach their potential so that they can make more significant contributions to the organization. As a servant leader, you must also recognize that it is your responsibility to do anything in your power to nurture and encourage the professional and personal growth of those around you.

No matter what age you are in or what generation you belong to, you are always searching for your purpose in the professional setting just like everyone else. If you want to see your organization and the people who work in it improve more and achieve success, you may want to practice this servant leadership along with all of its characteristics. When your employees see how committed you are to see them grow, they will feel more inspired and motivated. They will start believing in themselves more and as they see improvements, they will keep on doing their best for the good of the organization.

For most people, they focus on serving

themselves and their own interests when it comes to working. That is unless they have a more compelling reason to serve others. This is where your skills as a servant leader come into play. When you have a genuine commitment to your people, they will see you "in action" as you make it your purpose to serve them. In turn, they may feel encouraged to do the same.

Let's take another example to illustrate this. A servant leader of one department in the workplace will keep looking for and giving his team opportunities to move forward in their career. Because of this, the members of his team are more well-equipped to perform their tasks well and to come up with innovative ideas to improve their department. As the leaders of other departments see the improvements and success of this department, they can see how servant leadership can create a positive change. Because of this, they may ask for tips from the servant leader who, in turn, shares with them the wonders of this type of leadership.

Having a commitment to the growth of

people also allows servant leaders to build a culture of trust which gives employees the chance to shine. Often, a lot of leaders decide who to trust without even thinking about the people who trust them. Remember that trust must go both ways. If you place your trust in one of your employees but he does not really trust you, the situation might not turn out the way you want it to. Trust is an important part of commitment. So when your people see that you want them to grow and succeed, they know that you trust them and, in return, they end up genuinely trusting you too.

Building community

Servant leaders do not just love their own people or their own organization. They also love and work to improve the community. In fact, servant leaders must love their community more than their own success. You will never see a servant leader who sells out his community for any kind of flashy or immediate goals. Servant leaders also recognize the idea that the community has the ability to influence and shape lives in a positive way much more than corporate structures or other social systems.

As a servant leader, the final characteristic you must possess is building community. Recognize that in recent history, we have lost a lot because of the transition from the local communities to larger institutions as the main influencers of our lives. Recognizing this fact and being aware of it will cause you as a servant leader to try and identify a means to build community among the people who work in your organization. Servant leadership advocates that you can create a true community among your people and others who are employed at other organizations.

According to Greenleaf, all you need to build a community is yourself as a servant leader along with other servant leaders to help guide everyone. This is not done through mass movements. Instead, each of the servant leaders should demonstrate a limitless liability for a fairly specific group that is community-related.

The challenge of this characteristic is that it is a relatively "foreign concept" in corporations which are very business-minded. But the good news is that you can broaden building community as a characteristic to involve creating a sense of community among a group which interacts, lives, or works together. The leaders of these groups must help cultivate this sense of community by building a sense of fellowship. Among all of the characteristics of a servant leader, this one is probably the most important asset any organization may have.

If you want to better understand the laborious and long-term journey which communities must undergo for them to achieve maturity, you must look towards the steward of the community who, in this case, is the servant leader. As a servant leader, you need to be strong, dedicated, and effective if you want to create a strong community as well.

Even now, there are leaders all over the world who already possess this characteristic such as Suzi Nelson, Niki Vecsei, and Margot Mazur. Have you heard these names before? Anyone who's interested in Servant Leadership may have already come across the names of these powerful women. Suzi Nelson is the Community Manager of Digital Marketer. She openly provides her advocacy, support, assistance, and encouragement for the private customer group of her company. To do this, she bridges the gap between her company, the content they produce, and their customers. Since she started at the company herself, there has been an incredible increase in community activity thanks to her strategic method of building community.

Niki Vecsei is another well-known servant leader who also happens to be a highly experienced Social Media and Communities Engagement Manager with various content and digital marketing experience for a wide range of companies. Just like any other servant leader, she has a passion for connecting people, allowing everyone she works with to find success in their personal and professional lives. Although she's from Europe, she has experience working with a number of people across various countries in two continents.

As for Margot Mazur, she is currently the Senior Marketing Manager for Global Co-marketing Acquisition at HubSpot. She knows how to build strong and long-lasting communities and partnerships. She does this by connecting people to the necessary resources they need to produce their best work. As a leader, she focuses on products, partnerships, and growth. As you can see, these women are incredible examples of servant leaders who possess the important characteristics needed to create strong and long-lasting communities.

According to experts on servant leadership, building community also requires superior listening skills. And when you listen, you do not make judgments. At the beginning of Suzi Nelson's career, her job involved community and customer care. Since her focus was divided, she had to do more work in the long-run.

Instead of giving up, she spoke to her superiors and informed them that she could not focus on both tasks and do them to the best of her abilities. And so she placed all of her focus on community. She spent most of her time making her presence known in the group as part of the process of building community. Although she now admits that this was not the healthiest thing for her to do, creating that sense of community was extremely important to her so she persisted. Now, their culture of community has become solid and she finds things to be much easier.

Of course, building community may be a challenge in the beginning. But the more you work on it and the more you are able to establish this with your people, the easier it becomes. Then you can move on to learning and strengthening the other characteristics as your people work together as a community while encouraging others in the organization to do the same.

Now that you have learned about 10 important characteristics of Servant Leadership, wouldn't you like to know where your strength is. If you have not, follow the link *http://testyourleadership.site/* and take the quiz to assess your leadership.

Chapter 3: Servant Leadership in the Modern Business World

Yes, servant leadership has been around for so long now but it was only until Greenleaf emphasized its importance and coined the terms "servant leadership" and "servant leaders" did it become more well-known in this modern world. When it comes to servant leadership, you would invert the "power pyramid" so that you place the needs of your people over your own. This is the complete opposite of "traditional leadership" wherein leaders are placed at the very top of the power pyramid. But as a servant leader, you place emphasis on trust, growth, empathy, and collaboration.

Servant leadership is quite popular, especially in the industries which depend on highly-skilled employees. Also, servant leadership brings about a new type of social consciousness. Since its prevailing principle is that leaders exist in service of their people, this makes the organization serve the needs of its community. Now that we live in a world that is becoming more socially aware, applying servant leadership to the organization may help establish it as one which is authentic and ethical.

Apart from the characteristics we have discussed in the previous chapter, servant leaders also possess humility. This is one characteristic which a lot of leaders find challenging to learn. But if you want to become a good servant leader, you must recognize the input and skills of your people and see these of equal importance to your company as your own input and skills.

This is especially true for organizations which are knowledge-based. In such companies or industries, each employee may possess a special skill set which you cannot just replace. Always acknowledge the uniqueness of each employee no matter how "ordinary" they might seem. If you presume that you are the best person in the company and that your people are beneath you, there is very little chance that you will invest in them. Soon, you will start noticing a high rate of turnover in your company.

Humility is an essential trait of effective servant leaders, especially in this modern world. It is easy to feel knowledgeable and superior nowadays because there are so many resources available online. But no matter how much you think you know, there will always be people who know a little bit more than you. There will always be people who will not know as much as you but given the proper support, they will be able to excel in fields or jobs which you cannot seem to master. As a servant leader, you must acknowledge these facts and accept them if you want to grow and be able to serve others.

Servant leaders must also be authentic. You do not just serve others in order to look good. You can only become a true servant leader if you have a servant's heart. The desire to serve must come naturally. For people like this, they do not see their service as a chore. Instead, they believe that serving others is their purpose. And their people see this authenticity. As you read and learn more about servant leadership, you may want to apply it to your life as well. However, you must also know both sides of the coin.

Incredible as servant leadership may seem, not everyone believes in it. There are people who would raise their eyebrows at the thought of this type of leadership. They do not understand how they can become true leaders if they make it their purpose to serve others. Because of this, there is a chance that you might encounter some challenges on your journey towards becoming a servant leader.

The challenges associated with servant leadership

Wonderful as servant leadership is, making the choice to apply it to your own professional life comes with challenges. This is especially true in this modern world where most businesses are mostly driven by profits. More often than not, business owners only focus on making as much money as they can without thinking too much about the people who work for them.

Servant leaders are humble, never arrogant. They do not desire personal recognition instead; they feel more satisfied when they see their people succeed with their help. Such leaders are not afraid of pushing in different directions in order for them to make a significant impact to help their people grow and achieve success. They are not afraid of expressing their opinions and pointing out dysfunctions which other people see as uncomfortable and difficult to confront.

In any organization, when there is only one servant leader, this person has a very difficult road ahead of him. If this is a new concept to the organization, he will be met with skepticism, negativity, and even sarcasm. But an effective servant leader is not swayed by such challenges. If you want to become a servant leader, you must be aware of these challenges in order to prepare for them. Let's discuss them further:

☐ Servant leadership is nothing but a false premise

Most leaders believe that their main purpose is to serve their bosses, employers, and organization, not their people. Therefore, they believe that servant leadership is nothing but a false premise.

But the reality is, servant leaders also see themselves as followers in the overall scheme of things. Instead of focusing on their own success, they identify any gaps or issues which impede success and deal with them. They also encourage their people to recognize and address these issues while supporting and helping them as much as they can. Of course, this does not mean that they do not serve their superiors, employers, or the organization as well. Servant leaders have the desire to serve others, not just their people.

⚡ Servant leaders lack authority

Since servant leaders aim to serve others, there are some people who take advantage of this. Such people perceive their leaders as lacking the authority to get the job done. The more they see their leaders trying to cater to all of their needs, the less they see them as authoritative figures. What they do not see is that servant leaders are actually helping them succeed because they are looking at the bigger picture.

Of course, this does not mean that servant leaders have a fear of being authoritative. Notably, servant leaders are leaders too. But instead of using force, fear, or coercion, they use a serving approach in order to get the results they want.

For instance, an authoritative leader would force an employee to perform a task which he does not want to do. On the other hand, a servant leader would assign the task to an employee, ask the employee how he feels about the task, and would try to help him as much as he can. For one, the employee might not want to do the task because he does not possess the skills for it. So the servant leader would find a way to help this employee by giving him the proper training for him to acquire the skill. In the end, the servant leader helped his employee, the organization, and himself as well.

Rather than pushing their authority, servant leaders evaluate the current issues, conceptualize a vision for the company's future, inspire the team with this vision, and encourage the other superiors and managers to follow suit. Done properly, a servant leader will not have to assert his authority because the other people in the organization will follow him willingly.

▢ Servant leadership has a tendency to demotivate people

In some cases, employees might feel demotivated when their leaders are always stepping in to help. Some people take this the wrong way and they see this service as the leader not thinking that they are good enough. Because of this, the employees might start relaxing or exerting less effort because they know that their boss will resolve the conflict for them.

This is truly one issue which you have to be very careful with if you want to become a servant leader. Most employees already have their own preconceived notions about leaders and most of these notions are negative. So if you keep on trying to provide support, help or advice to your employees, they might take this the wrong way. Therefore, you need to show them that you believe in their abilities, but you are always there to help if they need it.

Also, you may allow them to perform the tasks to the best of their ability, acknowledge their efforts, and give some suggestions on how they can improve. It isall about communicating with your people. The more open you are with them, the more they will understand your willingness to serve without taking it the wrong way.

▢ **Servant leadership may limit one's vision**

Most leaders believe that they do not

have the time or that they should not invest too much of their time and efforts on their people as this might limit their vision. They must have a level of detachment from their employees so that they can resolve conflict, brainstorm ideas, explore new opportunities, and come up with an overall picture of the direction their department or organization is taking. And they can only do this by not bothering themselves with the needs of their people.

Of course, this is the exact opposite of servant leadership. Two of the main characteristics of servant leaders are foresight and conceptualization. This means that even though the servant leader serves his people and tries his best to meet their needs, this does not mean that he forgets to create a vision for his team or his organization. In fact, servant leaders are very much focused on their vision and all their actions point towards this vision. The more servant leaders help their people, the broader their vision becomes. They can see the potential of the people in the organization which means that they can create a vision which is far grander than the one they would have come up with as traditional leaders.

☐ Servant leadership focuses too much on the internal aspect

Some people claim that servant leaders focus too much on the introspection aspect of people. They keep encouraging their employees to look within themselves which, in turn, causes their work to suffer. Here is a picture some people may have in their mind about servant leaders: a servant leader is one who uses business meetings to discuss how meaningful their work is. However, this same leader does not formulate plans to increase profits and boost sales. This is because the leader does not focus on the outward aspect of business which is needed for the business to remain viable.

By now, you know that this is not true. Yes, servant leaders encourage their people to become more aware of themselves and to look at their inner strength. But this does not mean that they do not focus on the outside world as well. Servant leaders also know the workings of businesses. After all, they would not be placed in that position if they did not know anything about it! As a servant leader, you must learn how to balance the inner and outer aspects of your people, yourself, and your business. That way, you will be able to help your business grow while still being able to serve those around you.

Basically, servant leaders must learn how to minimize dysfunction and reduce conflict in a way that does not cause damage to the organization or to his people. Sometimes, when you try to meet the needs of everyone in order to keep them happy, this might lead them to go to and stay in their own comfort zone which is not a good thing either. This is another major challenge of servant leadership. Needless to say, true servant leaders will always find ways to develop and challenge their people so that they do not get too complacent. They help their people bolster their weaknesses while building on their strongest skills. This is why it isso effective.

However, even though servant leadership is so effective and has been proven to be highly successful, some leaders still do not believe in it. Of course, servant leadership is not perfect. Although you may find your way around certain issues, there will always be problems which you will find extremely difficult to fix. And just like any other leadership style or approach, servant leadership does come with its own set of disadvantages.

The disadvantages of the characteristics of servant leadership

As you can see, any challenge you would face on your journey towards becoming a servant leader is easily manageable. However, you would have to commit yourself to become a true servant leader in order to awaken your desire to serve others. Then the more you practice, the more you become better at being a true servant leader to your people. Of course, this does not mean that servant leadership only has advantages or benefits.

For instance, one of the most notable disadvantages of this leadership approach is that it isconsidered a "soft approach," which is not suited to a highly-competitive environment. In a world where you have to get everything done at the fastest possible time, servant leaders may have the tendency to lag behind traditional leaders when placed in a fast-paced and competitive setting.

Servant leaders focus more on encouraging, inspiring, and serving. Sometimes, this may lead to situations wherein responsibility and accountability are taken for granted. In the same way, many of the core characteristics of servant leaders might not be suitable for certain situations. Let's take a look at these characteristics once again and see how they can be a disadvantage for servant leadership.

Listening

Since servant leaders would like to listen to the opinions and suggestions of their people, it may take a longer time for decisions to be made. For instance, if as a servant leader, you want to get the input of all your people before making a final decision, this might work against you. In the business world, decisions must be made within a specific deadline. But if you focus too much on the listening aspect, this might end up slowing down the process of implementation which, in turn, can become a costly mistake in terms of revenue.

Empathy

For this characteristic, some servant leaders might experience something known as "empathy fatigue." This is especially true for those who have only started their servant leadership journey. As a servant leader, one of the ways you want to serve your people is by empathizing with them. However, empathy is not an unlimited resource. If you keep on empathizing with other people, this might end up draining you both emotionally and physically. Worse, it might even result in a burnout. And when this happens, you cannot be an effective leader to your people and your organization.

Healing

The disadvantage of this characteristic is very similar to the disadvantage of empathy. As a servant leader, you observe your people and see who are "broken" and thus, are in dire need of healing. However, if you focus too much on your people and not enough on yourself, healing might become a burden for you. Yes, you should put the needs of your people and your organization before your own. But not to the point that you have nothing left to give and you end up being the one who needs healing. Because, as sad as it is, other people might not be as keen on helping you heal as you were back when you still had the strength to heal others.

Awareness

Most servant leaders focus too much on the relational part of being a leader. They want to be aware of the people around them but in some cases, they forget that this is not the only important aspect of being a leader.

Although awareness is important, servant leaders must also focus on their own competence and skills in order to establish their authority. This authority is important if they want to distinguish their role in the organization.

Persuasion

When it comes to persuasion, a lot of people might take it the wrong way. If a servant leader tries to persuade his people to follow a certain process, this might end up making them less motivated. Although the servant leader has good intentions, his followers might not interpret them as such. If this kind of reaction continues over time, it might lead to a decrease in the productivity of the employees.

Also, the problem with persuasion is that some employees might perceive this negatively, especially when the servant leader always steps in to "improve" their work. Again, although the servant leader only wants to serve his people to make them better, they might take this the wrong way. Some people either think that their leader does not think they are good enough or that the leader does not accept or appreciate their efforts. Such thoughts can be very dangerous. Therefore, servant leaders must learn how to be persuasive in a positive and effective way.

Conceptualization

Unfortunately, another disadvantage of servant leadership is that it does not seem to fit all types of businesses. No matter how much you try to conceptualize the future or the vision of your organization, you must accept that this approach would take time for it to take effect throughout the organization. Not all leaders have the ability to conceptualize. If as a servant leader, you try to push this characteristic on them, they probably will not respond well to you.

Incredible as servant leadership is, it does come with a lack of stability which makes it very challenging for some leaders to implement. This is especially true for servant leaders who end up worrying too much about how their employees feel that they are not able to conceptualize properly.

Even when you try to come up with concepts to help your company succeed, when you think about how your employees will react, you start doubting yourself and the ideas you come up with.

Foresight

When it comes to servant leadership, foresight does not always work. No matter how much you try to predict what happens in the future of your company, employees and leaders in your organization might not be too keen on this approach you want to implement. In most cases, the servant leadership approach may require retraining in all the levels of the organization. But if you are the only leader in your company who is willing to use your foresight for the benefit of your company, you may have a challenging road ahead.

Stewardship

In the same way as the characteristic of foresight, no matter how much you would like to be the steward of your own organization, if you are the only one who wants to do this through steward leadership, then this can be a challenge. It would be like trying to sail a ship towards a destination while your whole crew is against it. So, you must have strength, commitment, and determination to improve your organization for the benefit of everyone.

Commitment to the growth of people

For this characteristic, the disadvantage is that servant leaders work against the traditions. If servant leaders want their people to grow and develop to the best of their abilities, they must accept the fact that they must surrender absolute authority. This means that they must go against the traditional structure of the corporate workplace. In order to allow your people to grow, you must involve them in the decision-making process which, unfortunately, is not okay for some organizations.

Building Community

Finally, this characteristic is not very compatible with traditional leadership styles which are more authoritative and directive. Servant leaders aim to serve their people as their priority. But when you look at this traditionally, your superiors might not agree with you on this. If their priority is to see you as a leader growing along with the organization, you might come into conflict with them. Since you focus more on your people, this might not sit well with how your employers want you to lead the organization.

Although servant leadership does come with its own disadvantages, this does not mean that you should not pursue it. No matter how bad things might seem, there will always be ways for you to overcome these challenges...

Overcoming the challenges and negativity

No matter what type of leader you choose to be, you cannot please everybody. This is one of the harsh realities of life which we have to deal with if we want to survive. Just because servant leadership comes with challenges, that does not mean that you should just give up and look for an easier route. The most important part is to stay strong so that you can overcome all of the challenges and negativity that come your way.

Servant leaders must learn how to balance the needs of their people and the goals of their organizations. Servant leaders are big picture thinkers which means that even while they serve their people, they are still able to foresee the goals of the organization. No company should ever neglect or ignore the needs of their employees. After all, without the employees, who will do the work? Although more leaders choose to be authoritarian or traditional, it takes a special kind of leader to be able to use the servant leadership approach successfully.

Learning how to become an effective servant leader is the most important aim of this book. Servant leadership does not necessarily mean that you will do everything your people ask of you. After all, you are still their leader. Instead, you should believe in the understanding and growth of people in order for you to serve them well. In some cases, servant leaders even make decisions which their people do not agree on as long as they know that their people will grow and learn from these decisions.

Anybody can become a servant leader. You can be one both in your personal and professional life. But when it comes to understanding servant leadership in the workplace, the CEO of the famous restaurant chain, Popeye's Louisiana Kitchen, Cheryl Bachelder explains it well. She wrote a book entitled "Dare to Serve" which inspires any would-be servant leader with the story of how the restaurant chain had transformed from a company on the brink of failing to one which experienced incredible growth in all aspects that matters to businesses. And all of this happened because the leaders of the company chose to incorporate servant leadership.

As Bachelder put it, a servant leader's ability to serve other people well and their success as leaders would first depend on how they perceive the people under their care. She also said that being a servant leader means that you consciously make a choice to become a leader who serves other people over their own self-interest.

One of the main problems with traditional leaders these days is that they have stopped seeing people from a "human perspective." But when you start seeing others as people who have the potential to grow and transform instead of merely focusing on their weaknesses and faults, you will be able to provide them with the encouragement and freedom they require in order to improve.

In her book, Bachelder also provides practical advice on how you can secure incredible performance from your people by inspiring them. She provides a description of how she and the other servant leaders in her team consciously chose to adopt a number of principles which are clearly defined. These principles are essential for servant leadership in order for people to deliver superior performance.

The principles they adopted are humility,

accountability, coaching, listening, passion, and planning. In her book, Bachelder provided a lot of inspiring stories and concrete examples of how they incorporated all of these essential principles. Just like this book, Bachelder's book is another excellent resource for anyone who aspires to become a true servant leader.

Before we move on to the ways you can overcome the challenges of servant leadership, try to have a moment of self-reflection first. When you hear the term "servant leadership," what does this make you think about? To you, what is a leader in this modern world? Why is it called servant leadership? Although servant leadership has been around since the ancient times, it has only become mainstream since Greenleaf coined the term. Since then, more and more modern leaders and companies have become interested in this concept.

As a leader, you have the ability to impact your people positively by serving them and inspiring them to make them better people. As a servant leader, you empower and enable other people to achieve success and reach their goals. If you already hold a leadership role and you want to take the same path as the other great servant leaders, you must learn how to be strong for your people.

You must accept that servant leaders aim to bring about the best in their people by instilling confidence, trusting them, and helping them improve. This applies when you are in the corporate world too. You must have passion for your people and for your organization in order to come up with a vision for the future. With this vision in mind, you can start empowering your employees so they can reach their full potential.

To start off, you need to acquire leadership skills which reflect the voice of an authentic servant leader. Acquire values which you can use to influence other people in order to create a safe and inspiring environment for them. Now let's move on to some practices you can employ to help you overcome the negativity and challenges surrounding servant leadership.

1. Find your voice

If you want to overcome the challenges of servant leadership, you must find your own voice. Leading and serving are separate entities. But an effective servant leader must master both. As a servant leader, you serve your people by leading them in such a way that they practice the essential qualities which merit trust. In order to gain the trust of other people, you must have your own voice and character that is relatable and authentic.

In order to do this, the first thing you must let go of is your ego. As you evolve to become a servant leader, you should also let go of any controlling and dictatorial tactics you used in the past. Keep in mind that when you introduce the "wrong" values to your people, this will affect their performance which, in turn, affects the whole organization as well. Although there is no such thing as a perfect leader, the thing which sets servant leaders apart is their ability to get rid of their ego in order to empower their people so that they can feel and see their own self-worth.

The key to becoming a servant leader who serves competently and with integrity is authenticity. Your people can always determine whether their leader is being authentic or not. So you must show them the strength of your character. If you want to gain the trust of your followers, you must also learn as much as you can about the vision of your company and the vision you have conceptualized for the company. In doing this, your people will feel more confident in your competence and willingness to build an excellent organization.

For a lot of people, finding their voice can be very challenging. But all great servant leaders are those who reaffirm their people's worth as you are trying to unite them as a team with a single vision. As time goes by, you will notice how incredible your people are and how they have also learned to discover their own voice. This becomes the fundamental culture of your company and it issure to bring you more success.

2. Empower each individual

Servant leaders are committed to their people. They provide opportunities to their people for growth and development in order to become better individuals and more efficient employees in the company. For traditional leaders, they impose their authority on their people just because they are the ones in power. In doing this, they are also suppressing the potential of their followers rather than lifting them up.

As challenging as servant leadership is, more people will see its value once you have started making a change for the better. Although other leaders may raise their eyebrows at your approach, when they see how the people on your team are growing professionally and are becoming more productive, this may enlighten them, especially if they cannot seem to push their teams or motivate them as well as you.

As a genuine servant leader, you will inspire each person in your team to reach for the dream and rise to the occasion. Empowered employees are those who recognize their own potential and understand their own purpose in the organization. When you enable your people to see and understand their worth, they are more inclined to use their talents and skills to achieve their goals for the overall success of the company. Empowering people also means influencing them positively. And in the end, the people who you once served as their leader are ready to become leaders as well.

3. Encourage others to serve just like you

After you have empowered your people and you have shown the other leaders in your organization how valuable servant leadership is, it istime to encourage them to do the same. If you are able to encourage others to serve just like you, this makes your whole organization stronger. It would be like creating a more meaningful sense of purpose which applies to everyone within your company. Once you have achieved this, the company as a whole can focus on carrying out the strategies of the company in order to achieve the main vision. After finding your own voice, you bring everybody together to have a single voice geared towards integrity, authenticity, and empowerment for a healthier and more inspiring corporate culture.

4. Work on your own effectiveness as a servant leader

For a lot of people, one of the biggest challenges they face is to work on their own effectiveness. From all of the characteristics to embody as a servant leader to learning all of the skills all great leaders require, there is surely a lot to learn. But if you do not want to stress yourself out, you should not rush yourself. There is no need to acquire all of these skills and characteristics right away.

The journey towards becoming a true servant leader is a continuous one. There is no "deadline" as you will be learning more and more each day. To help give you a structure to work with on your quest for servant leadership, consider these steps:

a. **Set achievable goals**: Leaders should make goal setting second nature. You should make yourself aware of where you want to be, what goals you want to achieve, and a timeline for your goals. This makes it easier for you to visualize what you want to achieve which, in this case, is becoming a more effective servant leader.

b. **Learn to prioritize**: As a leader, you will not have just one goal. You must set several goals for yourself, your people, and for the organization. The best way to do this is to learn how to prioritize. Categorize your goals then start prioritizing them. That way, you know which tasks are the most important and which one can be put off if needed.

c. **Delegate tasks as needed**: Although you are a leader, this does not mean that you should do all the work yourself. This does not empower your people and it does not help you in any way either. After prioritizing your goals, break them down further into achievable tasks. This makes it easier for you to see which work you can assign to your people and which work you must keep for yourself.

5. **Learn how to lead your team in the best way by serving them**

It isa lot easier to talk about servant leadership than it is to apply it. We have discussed the challenges and disadvantages in the previous sections and most of them boil down to other people not getting on board either because they do not understand servant leadership, or they feel skeptical towards it. Another way for you to overcome these challenges is to learn how to lead your team in the best way possible. Here are some strategies to help you out:

a. **Be an example**: The best way to show other people the effectiveness of servant leadership is by showing them how to do it and how effective it is. No matter how much you preach about servant leadership, people will not really "get it" unless they see results.

b. **Be intentional in your desire to serve**: Make it your intention and desire to coach, mentor, and develop other people. Take some time to listen to them, help them heal, and allow them to grow. The more you invest in others, the more benefits you will reap in the long-run.

c. **Learn more about your people and your organization**: Be aware of the strengths of each individual in your team. Then use those strengths to create a synergistic collection of individuals who deliver results constantly. As your team is growing and developing, learn more about your organization as a whole. This will help you see exactly how you can serve others outside of your team in the most effective way.

6. Always be there for your people to guide the change

As a servant leader, you must always be present for your people. We have discussed how servant leadership takes time. And if you do not want to get off track, make sure that you are the leader of the journey from the beginning. People will always have questions when changes happen. This is a normal thing.

Patiently answer those questions and keep guiding your people as genuinely as you can. The best time to start your servant leadership endeavor is the present. As soon as you have learned all that you can from this book, you can start thinking of ways to incorporate servant leadership into your life.

Communicate more with your people and involve them in the early decisions regarding the changes you want to make within your team. In the beginning, this will catch your people off guard, especially if you were more of a traditional leader in the past. But the more you involve your people, the more you communicate openly with them, the easier it will be for them to accept the change.

Also, do not get discouraged if you encounter resistance. Again, this is normal. Do not be like other leaders who perceive resistance as a negative thing. In fact, you should see resistance as something positive because it means that you are making real progress! If some of your people resist your ideas or strategies, do not start an argument with them. Cope with the situation while maintaining your principles and values. Listen to their opinions and try to understand what their concerns are so you can help them find the solution. You can even include this challenge in your plan so you can already think about ways to deal with it before it even happens!

Keep in mind that leadership is not just a role or a position, it isa choice. If you want to successfully carry out the mission and vision of your company, you have to start the journey yourself. If you are able to make servant leadership the core culture of your company, this means that you would have led your company in a path that leads to success.

Servant leadership is not just some vague concept. It is a real kind of leadership. It is wonderfully challenging, and it requires your self-direction, self-belief, and tenacity. It is all about challenging the norms and doing things differently from what people are used to, from what people normally accept. Prepare yourself for the criticism other people might throw at you, especially from those who have their own preconceived notions about what leadership should be. Be open but at the same time be firm to your goal.

Some people might have already learned about servant leadership but they may have had the wrong impression of it. Others might even shun you because they do not believe that serving those "beneath you" is not something worthy of leaders. But as long as you stick with what you believe in and you do not meet these negativities with anger or conflict, you do not have to worry about failing as a servant leader. After all, you can let your action say for yourself.

Remember that being a servant does not mean that you are "soft." In fact, the most famous servant leaders in the world have shown resilience, firmness, strength, and other powerful characteristics which makes those around them feel motivated to follow suit. So do not be afraid to serve your people and do not be afraid of the challenges. Sooner or later, you will see the fruits of your efforts in how incredible those around you are becoming.

Chapter 4: Developing Servant Leadership in Yourself

Servant leadership can come naturally to you if you are an empathic person. But even if empathy is not your strong suit, you can still become a servant leader. All people have their own strengths and weaknesses in terms of skills, capacities, characteristics, and more. If you want to become a servant leader, you should start developing the traits you need for it. Before doing this, you must first understand where you are right now.

After reading the earlier chapters of this book, you may want to start your servant leadership journey right away. Good for you! But for some people, it is not that easy. This is especially true for people who have learned the "traditional" way of becoming a leader and they do not know where to start. Those people have always led their people by asserting their authority so how do they start serving their people thinking of them as strange?

Servant leadership does not come without costs. For one, it would take you some time to apply the strategies, learn the characteristics, and also learn how to interact with others as a servant leader would. But if you really want your company to have servant leadership as part of its culture, there are many ways to do this. As previously mentioned, there is no better time to start than the present. If you want to become a servant leader, start as soon as possible. Do not keep putting things off. Start little by little but do it now. When you do this, you might realize that a lot of time has already passed, and you do not even remember how to start becoming a servant leader!

Anybody can become a servant leader. This endeavor may be smooth and simple to some but challenging and frustrating to others. Either way, have faith in yourself. No matter how hard things may seem, no matter how hard the situation may get, as long as you persevere you will start seeing powerful and positive changes happening in your organization.

We have spoken about some great servant leaders who have turned their companies around by learning how to serve others. Even now, there are people who have begun their servant leadership journey and who will become the greatest servant leaders of the future.

But how can you be one of these people? How can you start developing servant leadership within yourself? To start you off, consider these three effective methods which have been tried and tested by individuals and companies:

1. **Take inspiration from the servant leaders in the past and be an example for others**

    As a servant leader, you must inspire your people and the others around you to do the same. But how do you do this without being inspired yourself? There have been so many servant leaders in the past and in this modern world. Do research, learn more about them, and find inspiration in how they began their journey. Sometimes, you might have come across your past leaders who held some of the characteristics of servant leadership. Remember how they helped you grow and how you felt towards them. With your own inspiration, especially from your direct experience, you will feel more motivated to start your own journey and to stick with it no matter how many challenges you face.

More often than not, people learn things more profoundly through actions than through words. Think about it, how well will your people understand servant leadership when you simply explain it to them? Sure, some of them might be able to understand the concept but for others, they might just see this as nothing more than an idea which can never really happen.

Now how well do you think your people will understand servant leadership when you show them what a servant leader should be? Now that you know more about servant leadership, it is time to show others how it works. As your people see your desire to serve and your willingness to act on this desire no matter what other people say, they will have a more profound understanding of servant leadership. When this happens, you become their inspiration and they start learning from you.

2. Build a strong team consisting of servant leaders

The more you serve, the more your people will see you in service. The longer you do this, the more they will see how genuine your intentions are. When you serve others, they start learning how to serve as well. This creates a culture of service within your team and in the end, you will be able to build a strong team consisting of dedicated and genuine servant leaders.

There is nothing better than being able to unite a collection of people with diverse personalities, goals, and characteristics to work together towards a common goal. As you are learning to become the best servant leader you can be, you must also encourage each of your people to embrace and start practicing a culture of service each and every day.

The great thing about servant leadership is that the service you provide can come in a variety of forms. And you can apply all of these through the characteristics of servant leadership which are listening, empathy, healing, awareness, persuasion, conceptualization, foresight, stewardship, commitment to the growth of people, and community building. As you learn these characteristics and make them part of your everyday life, you will also learn to become a better servant leader as time goes by.

3. Keep on looking for opportunities to serve others

As aforementioned, servant leadership is not something that comes with a deadline. You can never say that you have become a servant leader and that is that. No matter how good you get, you should still continue providing service to those who need it. As you meet and interact with other servant leaders, you can learn more about servant leadership which you had not known or realized in the past.

Then you can start sharing this wonderful approach to others until all the other leaders and the people they lead have begun their own journeys toward servant leadership. As long as you keep on serving, you will be able to make a positive impact in your life and in the lives of those around you.

Practical tips to help you develop the characteristics of servant leadership

The three effective methods we have discussed in the previous section will help you develop servant leadership within yourself. Of course, there are other ways to do this too. In this section, we will go through some practical tips to help you learn and develop the most important characteristics of servant leadership. These tips can help anyone who is struggling in each area.

1. Listening

This characteristic is both easy and challenging. A lot of leaders know how to listen to others but how many of them actually, genuinely listen to what other people have to say? If serving is the core principle behind servant leadership, two of the main practices which can help you achieve this are asking questions and listening closely.

According to Darryl Spivey, one of the senior faculty members at CCL or the Center for Creative Leadership and is also a coach of servant leadership for executives, when you ask the right questions, it is like you are adding a "secret ingredient" to your recipe for great coaching. And this is also crucial for anyone who wants to become a servant leader.

As a servant leader, you must learn how

to build strong relationships with your staff and the best way to do this is by listening to them closely so that you actually hear and understand everything they say. To learn more about your people, you should ask them a lot of relevant questions. These questions cannot only help you learn about your people. You can also ask them questions during the process of decision-making so that they can give their own ideas and suggestions for the tasks at hand. And remember that sometimes what is not said can be as important as what is actually spoken, so you should keep listening to what is imply between the lines as well.

2. Empathy

The goal of empathy is to be able to understand the perspectives and experiences of other people. The first step towards empathy is to genuinely listen to the people around you. But this is not the only thing you must do as a servant leader. You should also learn to understand your own perspectives and prejudices. Then you must set these aside in order to broaden your ability to understand others.

Although some people naturally have this characteristic, others may have to work on it for them to learn it for servant leadership. Satya Nadella, the CEO of Microsoft whom we have mentioned earlier has talked about the importance of empathy in becoming an effective leader. He even wrote a book about this where he stated that empathy is going to become even more valuable when the world is taken over by technology and it starts causing disruptions in the status quo.

Servant leaders must always strive to understand and to share the thoughts and feelings of each person on their team. Listen to their explanation and try to imagine how you would think or react if you are in their shoes. You can also try giving your employees the benefit of the doubt, especially those whom you trust the most. When you always assume the good in your people, this will go a long way towards inspiring trust and loyalty in you by your people.

3. Healing

After learning how to listen and empathize with others, the next thing you may want to learn is how to help other people heal. In order for you to help others heal, you must first recognize that they need help. This applies to your people, to the other people in the organization, and to the organization as well. After that, you will be able to help them face challenges, achieve goals, or meet their needs to start their journey towards healing.

There are different ways in which you can help other people heal. If you notice someone in your team who has suddenly stopped working as hard, start a conversation with him. More often than not, people experiencing problems are notable to focus on their work as well as they could have. Asking your people about what they are going through is the first step towards healing. Then make them feel that you are willing to help them get through their struggles.

It is also an important step of listening, empathy, and servant leadership. When you are able to help your people heal, they can pick themselves up and start becoming productive again. And when all of your people have healed, you will see an improvement in the overall performance of your team which, in turn, will help the whole organization.

4. Awareness

You cannot become an effective servant leader if you are not aware of your followers and your organization. This is another core characteristic you need if you want to become an exceptional servant leader. Awareness refers to how well you are able to perceive the people around you. You should be well-informed and genuinely concerned about your people if you want to be aware of them.

To do this, you may want to learn more about them. And how do you learn more about your people? By listening to them. We always go back to the characteristic of listening because you need it to practice all the other skills and characteristics. The more you listen to your people, the more you become aware of them. Then you start learning about their skills, competencies, and more.

Another way to become more aware of your people is to take a genuine interest in them. Spend some time with your people both in and out of the workplace. While at work, take some time during your break to have "water cooler" conversations with your employees to gain more insight into them. Or you can invite your entire team out for dinner for a non-workplace-related bonding experience. The point of such exercises is to increase your interaction with your people in order for you to become more aware of them. At the same time, this can also be a good start to building a community.

5. Persuasion

Instead of using force, threats or other types of negative means to get results, servant leaders use persuasion. One of the most famous masters of persuasion was the late Steve Jobs, the founder of Apple. As a matter of fact, his people fondly spoke of Jobs' talent of persuasion. Apparently, he could persuade his people to meet deadline goals which were seemingly impossible!

Learning the art of persuasion is a key differentiating factor between servant leadership and traditional, authoritarian leadership. But how do you practice this skill? The most important component of this is dialogue. As you engage your people about an idea or concept which will benefit everyone and you work alongside them to make this happen, there is a higher likelihood that your people will develop an internal motivation they need to effectively perform their tasks.

So if you want to get better at persuading people, then you must keep on practicing. As a servant leader, you must lead your people using persuasion, not by using your raw authority. Use humor, logic, and other skills to sincerely persuade your people to follow your lead. In doing this, you engage them more effectively which, in turn, helps you to build strong relationships and mutual esteem.

6. Conceptualization

Remember that as a servant leader, you must always focus on the big picture. You should not allow yourself to get distracted by short-term goals or day-to-day operations. According to Richard Branson, the CEO of Virgin Media, it is alright to focus on the smaller details during the earlier stages of your business. However, you must also learn how to focus on the big picture which is your long-term goal.

One way to improve your conceptualization skill is to learn how to empower your people by allowing them to handle daily tasks. This will help free up your time so that you can start dreaming up and planning for a better future for your people and for the whole organization. Effective servant leaders have a profound understanding of all the aspects of business. In fact, only if you understand your business enough, that is when you know how you can guide your team to be effective in their day-to-day. Having the freedom to focus on your long-term goals while trusting your team to operate on their own also means that you have trustworthy and competent people.

Another strategy you can employ to develop conceptualization or big picture thinking is to have a reflection about how things "should" be in terms of the different areas of your business. Try to come up with a focused and specific vision that is clearly defined. This is an important step to take if you want things to change.

7. Foresight

As a leader, you may have already learned this skill. But foresight is slightly different when it comes to servant leadership. A unique way to improve your foresight to become a better servant leader is to interact more with people who are very different from you in terms of worldviews, gender, age, religion, race, and even national origin. When you talk to such people, you are able to learn more about their varying perspectives. In fact, they might be able to give you good ideas and concepts which you would never have thought of on your own.

Also, you may want to learn how to think systemically. Within any system, actions done in the present typically cause reactions or consequences in the future. Therefore, as a servant leader, you must learn how to hone your "systems thinking" skills which, in turn, helps you foresee the future in a better light. You will be able to foresee the likely outcomes of your decisions which allows you to build the future instead of just reacting to it.

You may also want to practice your

foresight by making well-considered predictions regularly. Then test these predictions against reality. You can even try creating a group exercise involving your people. Together, you can come up with predictions of important events or emerging trends related to your organization.

8. Stewardship

As a servant leader, you practice stewardship by focusing on others and taking responsibility for the resources you have at your disposal. When it comes to stewardship, this means that you show respect to all of the philanthropic resources given to you in order to achieve the objectives of your organization. This is not a learned behavior as much as it isa decision you make to take responsibility for other people (the people in your team) and their resources. Here, you focus more on the resources you have as a steward instead of you being a steward.

Remember that the resources at your

disposal are not really "yours." The organization entrusted these resources to you thus, you serve as a steward who will hold on to the resources, take care of them, and take responsibility for them, and use them as needed for the benefit of the organization in the long run.

Therefore, you must take your role as a steward seriously. Do not take things for granted as you might end up misusing the resources entrusted in your care. This is where conceptualization and foresight prove valuable. If you are able to come up with a vision and a prediction for the future of your organization, you can also come up with a plan wherein you utilize the resources given to you in the best way possible.

9. Commitment to the growth of people

For this characteristic, empowerment is key. You must always commit to the growth, development, and improvement of people. Remember that as a servant leader, you have a natural desire to serve others. You place their needs above your own as you want to see them reach their fullest potentials.

Sometimes this might mean that you will get results later as you let them figure out problems by themselves, but that is also a necessary step they need to take in order to learn in the long run. As a servant leader, many of the times your job involves thinking when you should help them and when you should let them swim on their own. It is crucial to do both. As when you let them come up with a solution themselves, you are empowering them with authority, while you make sure they are going the right path by guiding them. They will feel even more confident to learn and to try new ideas.

If you want to see your people grow, you must find ways to help them out. Most people feel content with where they are and what they have in terms of their professional life. Therefore, it is your responsibility as a servant leader to find ways to help your people move forward. One way you can do this is by looking for opportunities such as training, seminars, and the like, then encourage your people to attend. Or better yet, if you have the power to push an organization, incorporate the learning system. L'oreal is a very good example here. It provides their employees with a learning portal which educate, cultural and organizational content as well as expertise knowledge. L'oreal Employees also have access to any Coursera lessons for free so they can learn about any topics.

You can also help your people grow more effectively by getting to know them better, by becoming more aware of them as people. In doing this, you know exactly where your people need improvement. Although the members of your team may already be incredible at their jobs, there is always room to grow. So give them opportunities to learn new skills or to strengthen the skills which they feel are their weaknesses. Committing to the growth of your people makes your team stronger in the long-run.

10. Building community

If you are trying to think of a servant leader who passionately believes in this characteristic, you may want to learn more about the CEO of Unilever, Paul Polman. He believes that in such a community, both the customers and the employees can thrive. In particular, Unilever is very active in the emerging markets. For one, they have started an initiative known as "Perfect Villages" wherein they provide Unilever assistance to a thousand towns in Vietnam. The executives of the company stay for a whole week with poor families in the rural area to experience life among them. Polman shares that this initiative teaches their leaders to serve more effectively.

As a servant leader, you will not stop at serving your people. Once you have encouraged and inspired them to serve others as well, you can expand your scope and move on to the community. Come up with initiatives such as the example we have given. Having such activities gives the people in your organization a deeper understanding of what it is like to be true servant leaders. Doing this also helps your organization as the public becomes aware of your brand as one that is authentic, ethical, and is genuinely focused on serving others.

Making servant leadership your leadership style

More and more, you are learning practical tips on how to become an effective servant leader. At the beginning of this book, there is a link provided for you which you can use to evaluate your own servant leadership skills based on the 10 characteristics of servant leadership. By taking this quiz, you can focus on developing each of these characteristics better.

Servant leadership is, indeed, a powerful

leadership style. If you already hold a leadership role in your organization, it is time to start making servant leadership your leadership style. Here are more tips (and reminders) to help you out:

⬜ **Seriously listen to other people**

As you can see, listening will always be one of the most important parts of servant leadership. This is because you can never be a great servant leader unless you learn how to become an effective listener. You can even say that servant leadership begins with listening. Without this, you will not be able to practice the other characteristics and strategies to positively impact the lives of those around you.

⬜ **Offer your service willingly and happily**

Remember that servant leadership involves serving others. If you see this service as nothing more than a chore or obligation, it will not be effective at all. In order to have the true heart of a servant, you must always offer your help or service willingly and happily. Remember that servant leaders have a desire to serve others. This means that you want to do it and you are not being forced into it.

▢ Do not be afraid to do the "dirty work"

Being a servant leader means being willing to serve not just when it is convenient or easy. True servant leaders do not choose the type of service they provide. As long as someone needs help, servant leaders will be there to give it. Whether it is something easy like looking for training or other enrichment programs to something as challenging as helping clean up the community as part of the company's service, do not be afraid of serving others. Otherwise, you will not be able to become a truly effective servant leader.

▢ Provide recognition and credit where it is due

Another part of being a servant leader is providing recognition and credit to your people whenever they accomplish something. Remember that you are committed to their growth and improvement. So when you see them try their hardest and they are able to do great things because of this, do not deny them the credit they deserve. In fact, giving recognition is another way of empowering people. It keeps them motivated and inspired to keep on going no matter how challenging things get.

⟨?⟩ **Always be present when you can**

Finally, always be there for your people and for your organization whenever you can. As a leader, you should not choose the people or the relationships to focus on. No matter how strong, how empowered, or how weak the person is, you should be present with and for them. This is another thing servant leaders do. When you think about it, how can you serve when you are not really there for your people? It is as simple as that.

With all of these helpful and practical tips,

becoming a servant leader will not be as much of a challenge anymore. As part of your service to others, you may want to leave a positive review for this book to share with others how useful and helpful it is. That way, you can spread the message about servant leadership to other leaders who are planning to start their own quest towards becoming a servant leader in their organization.

Is this something you feel useful? I hope you do. Share your honest thoughts about it in the review because I value my readers' insights.

Chapter 5: Servant Leadership for Non-Leaders

Servant leadership does not just apply to leaders. Even if non-leaders can start learning how to become servant leaders. Servant leadership as a concept is pretty intuitive. As a matter of fact, you may already be practicing it without even knowing it!

Think about this: do you focus on identifying the needs of others? Do you try to listen and understand why they need what they need? Once you have identified these needs, do you try to meet them instead of trying to become wealthy, powerful, and famous? If you have answered "yes" to both of these questions, then you are already on your way to become a servant leader.

Servant leadership does not just apply to the corporate or professional setting. You can practice it in other aspects of your life as well. Keep in mind that servant leaders always focus on the needs of others and thus, they become more effective leaders. Therefore, if you are a non-leader but you plan to become one in the future, you can immediately start as an effective servant leader.

One of the core characteristics of servant leaders is being excellent listeners. Anybody can determine whether they can be servant leaders or if they only focus on serving their own interests just by how well they listen to others. No matter how brilliant or talented you are, if you do not know how to genuinely listen to others, you will not be able to become a good servant leader. So you should learn how to interact properly with others and listen to them, really listen to them in order to gain a better understanding of who they are as persons and what their most pressing needs are. Only then can you be able to help them in the most significant way possible.

For non-leaders, the best way to adopt servant leadership is to start as early as possible. The moment you decide to become a leader in an organization or the moment you decide to start your own organization, you should incorporate servant leadership at the very core. Make this one of the founding values of your role or of your organization. This makes it easier for you to become a true servant leader from the beginning.

Remember to remain introspective at all times. Learn more about yourself first before you can start serving other people. Know your own strengths and your own weaknesses so that you can determine exactly how you can positively affect those around you. Even as a non-leader, you can learn how to become a servant leader for yourself and for those around you.

Anyone can be a leader!

Servant leadership is considered a paradoxical concept which has been around since the times of Jesus and Lao Tzu. And in this modern world where we are all in desperate need of fresh leadership approaches and new leaders, this is the perfect time to adopt this paradoxical concept which has proven to be highly effective.

In order to unleash transformative change in the form of servant leadership, we must start developing servant leaders who will not be afraid of transforming the conventional systems. As a servant leader, you must learn how to transform yourself, encourage the people around you to do the same along with the organization you are leading. Ultimately, this will allow you to influence the community which your organization is serving too.

Although some people do not believe in servant leadership because it is a paradoxical concept, this is precisely what you should expect from a leadership approach modeled by the greatest servant leaders in the world. When Greenleaf coined the terms in the past, he purposely chose these paradoxical terms (servant leaders and servant leadership) because they perfectly exemplified the paradoxical nature of this leadership style.

Traditionally, leaders aim to succeed in order to gain power, wealth, and fame. But this is not the case for servant leaders who first desire to serve before they lead. They do not force others to serve them. They are more interested and focused on giving rather than receiving. Servant leaders are stewards who aim to give back to their people, their organization, and their community.

If you want to become a servant leader, you must get rid of the idea that leaders only control people and command them to do their bidding. Such leaders are not interested in listening to the ideas, interests, or needs of their people or of anyone else for that matter. They might have the nerve to refer to themselves as "public servants" but in reality, they only serve for their own benefit. They do not have the humility to truly understand that leaders need their people as much as their people need them.

With all the benefits and good servant leadership has to offer, it is no wonder why more and more people are getting interested in it. You have already learned a lot about servant leadership and how you can start embarking on this life-changing journey. The next step is to start employing the tips and strategies you have learned. From then on, the journey becomes a learning process in itself. As you reap the rewards, you also gain new insights and information about true servant leadership.

Practical tips any non-leader can use

Not all leaders are born, some of them are made. Even as a non-leader, you can start learning about servant leadership and gradually incorporate its principles, philosophy, and strategies into your own life. Here are some important tips to help you out if you want to improve yourself as preparation to become a great servant leader:

◻ **Focus more on service instead of perfection**

Servant leadership is not just a buzzword which you use to describe your leadership style just to impress people. Neither is it something which you can master overnight. It is actually a way of life which requires commitment and a lot of conscious thought. Of course, you must also keep in mind that even though you have started on the path of servant leadership and you come into an organization as a servant leader, this does not guarantee that you will be a perfect leader.

No matter how well you learn the principles and characteristics of servant leadership, you will never be a perfect leader and that is okay. Nobody is perfect and nobody expects you to be perfect. The best you can do is focus on service and be as authentic as you can to your people. This will go a long way in terms of getting your people to trust you so you can build strong, profound relationships with them.

⯀ Practice compassion

The Dalai Lama, also known as Tenzin Gyatso is one of the greatest servant leaders to have ever existed. He is the temporal and spiritual servant leader of the Tibetan people. Since arriving in India where he started the Central Tibetan Administration, he has served tirelessly in order to achieve a self-governing democracy in Tibet. While doing this, he is also actively sharing his message of compassion and peace with the rest of the world.

If you want to become a great servant leader, you must attune yourself to the concerns and needs of your people. Learn how to listen compassionately to others. Take the time to hear what other people have to say and be as genuine as possible when you are trying to understand their message.

Being compassionate is also an important part of persuasion. Your people will know if you are just trying to get them to do what you want. But when your people feel that genuine compassion for you, it is easier to get them to trust you. In turn, it is also easier for them to get on board when you are trying to persuade them of something.

☐ Observe and learn from the great servant leaders of the past and present

Another way you can learn how to become a servant leader is to try and observe all kinds of leaders and how their decisions and actions affect their people and their organization. Aside from learning all about servant leadership from books and articles, seeing it in real-life through the examples of great servant leaders will help you understand better what it is all about.

Take Nelson Mandela, for instance. This great man lived most of his life experiencing ethnocentric antagonism, violence, and racism which ended after his imprisonment which lasted for 27 years! Despite this, when Mandela was released from prison, he went out into the world campaigning for reconciliation and peace with the white people.

He served as a leader for his people and he fought for their rights rather than thinking of his own welfare. Instead of thinking of his own needs, Mandela looked at the big picture. He had great foresight which helped him end the cycle of violence which plagued his people for years.

This is just one example of a great leader who was not afraid to go against the norm in order to fight for and empower his people. We have also talked about other servant leaders in the past chapters and if you try to recall, they all were able to make a significant positive impact in the lives of their followers and of the people around them. Learn from these great leaders and you will definitely be on the right path towards servant leadership.

▢ Learn how to nurture others

When you ask people to think of a servant leader who was very nurturing, most of them would probably think of Mahatma Gandhi, another great man.

He is well-known all over the world as the "Father of India" who always resorted to non-violence. This servant leader had a sense of empathy and compassion along with a strong desire to heal other people. All of these characteristics combined make for one incredible nurturer.

So if you want to become a servant leader much like Gandhi, you must learn what it takes to nurture others. When you are placed in a leadership position, look at your people as human beings who need to be nurtured and cared for so that they can grow, improve, and reach their goals. In doing this, your people will learn to love you, appreciate you, and draw inspiration from you.

▢ Focus on building strong relationships with your people

Finally, you should also focus on creating strong and long-lasting relationships. Think of your people as an investment. In doing this, you will find it easier to commit to their growth and to build a community which starts with them. When it comes to helping people, this does not mean that you do everything for them. Instead, it means that you should give them opportunities to learn and grow but allow them to go through the process on their own.

Also, you must recognize the value of each person on your team. All jobs, no matter how small, are important. Focus on the strengths of your people and soon, you will see them becoming better versions of themselves. This, in turn, helps your team improve and grow as a whole.

The bottom line is this: whether you are a leader or not, you can learn how to become a servant leader. Arming yourself with information about servant leadership is an important step. But you should also focus on practicing and applying the information you have learned in your life. This will help you become the servant leader you want to be!

Conclusion

The strength of a business organization largely depends on the soundness of its business model and leadership. Visionaries, challengers, and game-changers have led successful organizations because they held firm to specific principles embedded in their leadership styles and in the business models they used.

Whether your business will be a dominant player in the next five or ten years, is a question that can best be answered by looking inward at a personal and organizational level. Servant leadership is the key that opens doors to robust employee performance, exponential growth and unprecedented bottom lines.

Senior executives, intrapreneurs, entrepreneurs, investors, consultants, designers, and many other professionals have reaped massively from servant leadership. When you strive to empower your followers, they reciprocate by becoming more loyal, positive and always motivated.

Embracing diversity and personal responsibility is at the core of servant leadership. With today's organizations drawing employees from around the world, diversity cannot be avoided. Through servant leadership, you can cultivate an atmosphere where each one feels appreciated irrespective of their background. This brings cohesion in organizations.

People that are well-cultured through servant leadership frameworks bear personal responsibilities and take charge of their day to day assignments. Such self-driven and ambitious people are what organizations need to succeed in the current business environment.

When you realize that your human resource base is the gateway to creating value and delivering the same to your target customers through key relationships, you will do anything to care and nurture this most important resource. People are not cogs in the wheels of business; they are life-carrying agents endowed with explosive power to transform your organization into a number one business in whichever field. However, uncorking this potential requires servant leadership.

Interestingly the concept of servant leadership is not the preserve of leaders only. Even aspiring leaders can begin learning and digesting what it takes to be true servant leaders. Looking at the needs of others around you, helping your colleagues at work to get through tough circumstances and celebrate as a team is what servant leadership is all about. You get to practice it in your own space at your own pace.

With business dynamics changing and stakeholders demanding more than just per share earnings reports and dividends, sustainability reports are gaining prominence in boardrooms. What organizations are doing to cultivate positive work cultures, encourage professionalism and ethics while upholding the human element is increasingly gaining traction.

Through a simple leadership audit, you can find out the style or theory of leadership your organization is patterned after. Once you know this, you can begin a reorientation journey towards servant leadership. It may not happen overnight; Rome was not built in a day. Every step you make draws you closer to the epicenter of servant leadership.

Success leaves footprints and this is truer in leadership more than anywhere else. The world is not short of organizations and people who've walked down this road and left marks along the way. Through principles as basic as the art of listening you can begin tapping into the transformative power of servant leadership.

As you build strong relationships with your team, they too will extend the bridge to build even stronger relationships with your customers and other stakeholders. Customer acquisition, retention, and upselling are all spokes whose hub is the human resource. Without a team that is trained, guided and given space to explore possibilities without prejudice, customer relationships cannot be fully established.

When customers see the authenticity of the people they are dealing with, their loyalty index goes up. Servant leaders are authentic in and of themselves. They have a bias towards action and help others to surmount personal and organizational challenges by lifting them from their dugouts.

Even though servant leaders lower themselves to the level of their followers, they maintain their vision. This is important to avoid being consumed by the exigencies of the situation leaders find their followers in. Maintaining your focus on the bigger picture is the leadership part of the paradox while identifying with your employees' emotions and current circumstances is the servant bit of it. You need both to succeed.

Companies are mirror images of the kind of leaders they have. Effective leadership encourages collaboration and fosters a shared sense of purpose. For this to happen, the leader is centrally tasked with the responsibility of developing other leaders. This is achieved by creating an environment that enhances employees' abilities to take on decisions and create change. As Max DePree, an American businessman and writer clearly put it: "The signs of outstanding leadership appear primarily among the followers."

Servant leaders know how to embrace change as an opportunity and not a threat. They have a diagnostic ability to understand where a change of approach is needed in dealing with people and behavioral flexibility to change tact as and when required.

They know the value of porous and permeable boundaries in their bid to get information from their immediate environment. For this reason, they do not struggle relating with people at the periphery or at the bottom of the pyramid as these are the most creative yet the least consulted.

If you want to be a transformative servant leader tomorrow, begin today by spending much of your time nurturing others. The 21st-century business environment is unforgiving; leaders need a hawk-eyed clarity on what is important to their business and stakeholders in the long term. There is a need for a clear vision and meaningful strategic intent.

All this is achievable for all organizations across space and time provided they have the right servant leadership framework firmly in place. Servant leaders will help remind and steer the team towards what is important and create an enabling environment where people exercise their abilities and test possibilities without the fear of being dwarfed by the clenched iron fist of autocracy and insensitive leadership.

If you enjoy the content of this book, please do leave your review. I'd love to hear what my book can do for readers. If you do not like it, leave your review too so I can make the book better for other readers.

Bibliography

Bizfluent. (2019). *How to Practice Servant Leadership.* [online] Available at: https://bizfluent.com/how-4786254-practice-servant-leadership.html [Accessed 19 Apr. 2019].

Cleverism. (2019). *Servant Leadership Guide: Definition, Qualities, Examples, and More.* [online] Available at: https://www.cleverism.com/servant-leadership-guide/ [Accessed 19 Apr. 2019].

Forbes.com. (2019). *Council Post: Servant Leadership: How To Put Your People Before Yourself.* [online] Available at: https://www.forbes.com/sites/forbescoach escouncil/2017/07/19/servant-leadership-how-to-put-your-people-before-yourself/#7ff9fb6266bc [Accessed 19 Apr. 2019].

Forbes.com. (2019). *Who Is The Servant Leader Really Serving?.* [online] Available at: https://www.forbes.com/sites/katecooper/2018/07/03/who-is-the-servant-leader-really-serving/#3e48c4a0323c [Accessed 19 Apr. 2019].

Greenleaf Center for Servant Leadership. (2019). *What is Servant Leadership? - Greenleaf Center for Servant Leadership.* [online] Available at: https://www.greenleaf.org/what-is-servant-leadership/ [Accessed 19 Apr. 2019].

Inc.com. (2019). *10 Compelling Reasons Servant Leadership May Be the Best, Says Science.* [online] Available at: https://www.inc.com/marcel-schwantes/10-convincing-reasons-to-consider-servant-leadership-according-to-research.html [Accessed 19 Apr. 2019].

Investopedia. (2019). *What Is Servant Leadership?.* [online] Available at: https://www.investopedia.com/articles/financialcareers/10/servant-leadership.asp [Accessed 19 Apr. 2019].

Mackey, Z. (2019). *Everything You Need to Know About Servant Leadership.* [online] Ideas.bkconnection.com. Available at: https://ideas.bkconnection.com/everything

-you-need-to-know-about-servant-leadership [Accessed 19 Apr. 2019].

Mindtools.com. (2019). *Servant LeadershipPutting Your Team First, and Yourself Second.* [online] Available at: https://www.mindtools.com/pages/article/servant-leadership.htm [Accessed 19 Apr. 2019].

Mr Clarke's Blog. (2019). *Advantages and Disadvantages of Servant Leadership.* [online] Available at: https://5j16mrclarke.wordpress.com/2016/01/16/advantages-and-disadvantages-of-servant-leadership/ [Accessed 19 Apr. 2019].

Sivasubramaniam, J. (2019). *5 Companies That Embrace Servant Leadership.* [online] Ideas.bkconnection.com. Available at: https://ideas.bkconnection.com/five-surprising-companies-that-embrace-servant-leadership [Accessed 19 Apr. 2019].

Smallbusiness.chron.com. (2019). *Problems With the Servant Leadership Model.* [online] Available at: https://smallbusiness.chron.com/problems

-servant-leadership-model-50586.html [Accessed 19 Apr. 2019].

St. Thomas University Online. (2019). *What is Servant Leadership?*. [online] Available at: https://online.stu.edu/articles/education/what-is-servant-leadership.aspx [Accessed 19 Apr. 2019].

Toservefirst.com. (2019). *Definition of Servant Leadership*. [online] Available at: http://toservefirst.com/definition-of-servant-leadership.html [Accessed 19 Apr. 2019].

When I Work. (2019). *The Ultimate Guide to the Servant Leadership Model - When I Work*. [online] Available at: https://wheniwork.com/blog/the-ultimate-guide-to-the-servant-leadership-model/ [Accessed 19 Apr. 2019].

Cherylbachelder.com. (2019). [online] Available at: https://cherylbachelder.com/servant-leadership/traits-of-servant-leaders-foresight/ [Accessed 19 Apr. 2019].

CLA. (2019). *Is Steward Leadership Different than Servant Leadership?*. [online] Available at: https://christianleadershipalliance.org/blo g/2013/07/10/steward-leadership-servant-leadership/ [Accessed 19 Apr. 2019].

Fox, M. (2019). *Servant Leadership Characteristics and Why They Are Effective*. [online] Ideas.bkconnection.com. Available at: https://ideas.bkconnection.com/servant-leadership-characteristics-and-why-they-are-effective [Accessed 19 Apr. 2019].

Fresh Business Thinking. (2019). *Servant Leadership, Empathy and Healing | Fresh Business Thinking*. [online] Available at: https://www.freshbusinessthinking.com/se rvant-leadership-empathy-and-healing/ [Accessed 19 Apr. 2019].

Greenleaf Center for Servant Leadership. (2019). *Listen to Serve: Servant Leadership and the Practice of Effective Listening - Greenleaf Center for Servant Leadership*. [online] Available at: https://www.greenleaf.org/listen-to-serve-servant-leadership-and-the-practice-of-effective-listening/ [Accessed 19 Apr. 2019].

Grocer.coop. (2019). *Servant Leadership and Cooperation | Co-op Grocer Network.* [online] Available at: https://www.grocer.coop/articles/servant-leadership-and-cooperation [Accessed 19 Apr. 2019].

Linkedin.com. (2019). *Empathy as a Crucial Leadership Competency for Servant Leaders.* [online] Available at: https://www.linkedin.com/pulse/empathy-crucial-leadership-competency-servant-leaders-bawany/ [Accessed 19 Apr. 2019].

Linkedin.com. (2019). *Self-awareness is Critical to Servant Leadership.* [online] Available at: https://www.linkedin.com/pulse/self-awareness-critical-servant-leadership-knutson-mba-cplp-cm/ [Accessed 19 Apr. 2019].

Regent.edu. (2019). [online] Available at: https://www.regent.edu/acad/global/publications/jvl/vol1_iss1/Spears_Final.pdf [Accessed 19 Apr. 2019].

The 16%. (2019). *The Servant Leader and Awareness.* [online] Available at: https://the16percent.com/2014/05/14/the-servant-leader-and-awareness/ [Accessed 19 Apr. 2019].

The 16%. (2019). *The Servant Leader and Conceptualization.* [online] Available at: https://the16percent.com/2014/06/11/the-servant-leader-and-conceptualization/ [Accessed 19 Apr. 2019].

The 16%. (2019). *The Servant Leader and Foresight.* [online] Available at: https://the16percent.com/2014/05/28/the-servant-leader-and-foresight/ [Accessed 19 Apr. 2019].

The 16%. (2019). *The Servant Leader as a Healing Influence.* [online] Available at: https://the16percent.com/2014/05/07/the-servant-leader-as-a-healing-influence/ [Accessed 19 Apr. 2019].

The 16%. (2019). *The Servant Leader as Empathetic.* [online] Available at: https://the16percent.com/2014/04/30/the-servant-leader-as-empathetic/ [Accessed 19 Apr. 2019].

The 16%. (2019). *The Servant Leader as Persuader.* [online] Available at: https://the16percent.com/2014/05/21/the-servant-leader-as-persuader/ [Accessed 19 Apr. 2019].

Ayres, C. (2019). *7 Advantages and Disadvantages of Servant Leadership.* [online] ConnectUS. Available at: https://connectusfund.org/7-advantages-and-disadvantages-of-servant-leadership [Accessed 19 Apr. 2019].

Bright Hub. (2019). *Servant Leadership Theory Strengths and Weaknesses.* [online] Available at: https://www.brighthub.com/office/home/articles/73511.aspx [Accessed 19 Apr. 2019].

CMX. (2019). *How Do You Lead a Community? The 6 Common Characteristics of Servant Leadership in Communities.* [online] Available at: https://cmxhub.com/how-do-you-lead-a-community-the-6-common-characteristics-of-servant-leadership-in-communities/ [Accessed 19 Apr. 2019].

CMX. (2019). *How Do You Lead a*

Community?   The   6   Common Characteristics of Servant Leadership in Communities. [online] Available at: https://cmxhub.com/how-do-you-lead-a-community-the-6-common-characteristics-of-servant-leadership-in-communities/ [Accessed 19 Apr. 2019].

Hagelin, R. (2019). - *The Challenge: Servant Leadership.* [online] Townhall. Available   at: https://townhall.com/columnists/rebeccah agelin/2015/03/12/the-challenge-servant-leadership-n1969297 [Accessed 19 Apr. 2019].

HuffPost. (2019). *Being a Servant Leader in the Age of Technology.* [online] Available at: https://www.huffpost.com/entry/being-a-servant-leader-in-the-age-of-technology_b_8016290 [Accessed 19 Apr. 2019].

Leaderonomics.com. (2019). *The Pitfalls Of Servant Leadership.* [online] Available at: https://leaderonomics.com/leadership/the-pitfalls-of-servant-leadership [Accessed 19 Apr. 2019].

Linkedin.com. (2019). *The Challenges of Servant Leadership.* [online] Available at: https://www.linkedin.com/pulse/challenges-servant-leadership-paul-whiteside/ [Accessed 19 Apr. 2019].

Modern Servant Leader. (2019). *Servant Leadership - Modern Servant Leader - Serving First.* [online] Available at: https://www.modernservantleader.com/servant-leadership/servant-leadership/ [Accessed 19 Apr. 2019].

Official Blog - Australian Institute of Business. (2019). *Servant leadership in the modern workplace.* [online] Available at: https://www.aib.edu.au/blog/leadership/servant-leadership-in-the-modern-workplace/ [Accessed 19 Apr. 2019].

Pencak, S. (2019). *How To Overcome Today's Top Leadership Challenges | Silvia Pencak.* [online] Silvia Pencak. Available at: https://silviapencak.com/overcome-top-leadership-challenges/ [Accessed 19 Apr. 2019].

Sites.psu.edu. (2019). *Challenges of Servant Leadership.* [online] Available at:

https://sites.psu.edu/leadership/2013/11/1
1/challenges-of-servant-leadership/
[Accessed 19 Apr. 2019].

Smallbusiness.chron.com. (2019). *Problems With the Servant Leadership Model.* [online] Available at: https://smallbusiness.chron.com/problems -servant-leadership-model-50586.html [Accessed 19 Apr. 2019].

Wilson, A. (2019). *Servant Leadership Leads to Support for Community.* [online] Sites.psu.edu. Available at: https://sites.psu.edu/leadership/2014/11/0 6/servant-leadership-leads-to-support-for-community/ [Accessed 19 Apr. 2019].

Yourbusiness.azcentral.com. (2019). *Problems With the Servant Leadership Model.* [online] Available at: https://yourbusiness.azcentral.com/proble ms-servant-leadership-model-6795.html [Accessed 19 Apr. 2019].

Ainomugisha, G. (2019). *Your Complete Guide to Servant Leadership.* [online] The 6Q Blog. Available at: https://inside.6q.io/servant-leadership-guide/ [Accessed 19 Apr. 2019].

Boogaard, K. (2019). *Servant Leadership: What it is and Why it Matters - Toggl Blog*. [online] Toggl Blog. Available at: https://blog.toggl.com/servant-leadership/ [Accessed 19 Apr. 2019].

Clayton, M. (2019). *How to Manage with Servant Leadership - ProjectManager.com*. [online] ProjectManager.com. Available at: https://www.projectmanager.com/blog/manage-servant-leadership [Accessed 19 Apr. 2019].

Ebener, D. (2019). *On Becoming a Servant Leader*. [online] Sojourners. Available at: https://sojo.net/magazine/february-2011/becoming-servant-leader [Accessed 19 Apr. 2019].

Forbes.com. (2019). *Think Servant Leadership Is Too Good To Be True? Why It isThe Best Investment A Business Can Make*. [online] Available at: https://www.forbes.com/sites/davidkwilliams/2016/08/02/think-servant-leadership-is-too-good-to-be-true-why-its-the-best-investment-a-business-can-make/#2ca4485e79e1 [Accessed 19 Apr. 2019].

Iarocci, J. (2019). *Servant Leadership – 7 Ways to Cultivate Foresight.* [online] Cairnway Center For Servant Leadership in the Workplace. Available at: https://serveleadnow.com/servant-leadership-7-ways-cultivate-foresight/ [Accessed 19 Apr. 2019].

Inc.com. (2019). *How to Become a Servant Leader.* [online] Available at: https://www.inc.com/guides/2010/08/how-to-become-a-servant-leader.html [Accessed 19 Apr. 2019].

Leadership-Central.com. (2019). *Servant Leadership Style.* [online] Available at: https://www.leadership-central.com/servant-leadership-style.html [Accessed 19 Apr. 2019].

One Another Ministries. (2019). *Communication Tips for Servant Leaders: 6 Ways That Learning Styles Help Your Listeners Hear You - One Another Ministries.* [online] Available at: http://christianleadership.org/communication-tips-for-servant-leaders-6-ways-that-you-can-help-your-listeners-hear-you/ [Accessed 19 Apr. 2019].

Our State of Generosity. (2019). *Developing Skills as a Servant Leader in a Nonprofit.* [online] Available at: http://ourstateofgenerosity.org/how_to/developing-skills-servant-leader-nonprofit/ [Accessed 19 Apr. 2019].

SHRM. (2019). *The Art of Servant Leadership.* [online] Available at: https://www.shrm.org/resourcesandtools/hr-topics/organizational-and-employee-development/pages/the-art-of-servant-leadership.aspx [Accessed 19 Apr. 2019].

Smale, T. (2019). *'Servant Leadership' and How Its 6 Main Principles Can Boost the Success of Your Startup.* [online] Entrepreneur. Available at: https://www.entrepreneur.com/article/307923 [Accessed 19 Apr. 2019].

Smallbusiness.chron.com. (2019). *How Do I Improve Leadership Listening Skills?.* [online] Available at:

https://smallbusiness.chron.com/improve-leadership-listening-skills-2968.html [Accessed 19 Apr. 2019].

The Systems Thinker. (2019). *From Hero as Leader to Servant as Leader - The Systems Thinker.* [online] Available at: https://thesystemsthinker.com/from-hero-as-leader-to-servant-as-leader/ [Accessed 19 Apr. 2019].

Toservefirst.com. (2019). *Key Practices of Servant-Leaders.* [online] Available at: http://toservefirst.com/key-practices-of-servant-leadership.html [Accessed 19 Apr. 2019].

Alder Koten. (2019). *5 Reasons Why You Should Switch to the Rare Servant Leadership - Alder Koten.* [online] Available at: https://alderkoten.com/5-reasons-why-you-should-switch-to-the-rare-servant-leadership/ [Accessed 19 Apr. 2019].

Forbes.com. (2019). *Are You Ready To Become A Servant Leader?.* [online] Available at: https://www.forbes.com/sites/sallypercy/2

018/08/02/are-you-ready-to-become-a-servant-leader/#888fb56bc7d6 [Accessed 19 Apr. 2019].

Leaderonomics.com. (2019). *Famous Servant Leaders And How To Lead Like Them.* [online] Available at: https://leaderonomics.com/leadership/lead-like-famous-servant-leaders [Accessed 19 Apr. 2019].

Leadership Inspirations. (2019). *9 Ways To Be A Better Servant Leader - Leadership Inspirations.* [online] Available at: https://leadershipinspirations.com/2018/04/16/9-ways-to-be-a-better-servant-leader/ [Accessed 19 Apr. 2019].

3 Studies Prove Servant Leadership Good for Business - Modern Servant Leader. (2019). Retrieved from https://www.modernservantleader.com/servant-leadership/studies-prove-servant-leadership-good-business/

(2019). Retrieved from https://characterandcitizenship.org/images/cherp/presentations/Servant_Leadership_for_C_06-2015Rev1DSO2.pdf

Cheryl Bachelder: Servant Leadership is a model for performance. (2019). Retrieved from https://www.youtube.com/watch?v=It3Pw nvm5mk

Dr. Robert Liden "How Servant Leadership Improves Business Performance". (2019). Retrieved from https://vimeo.com/95023921

Hu, J., & Liden, R. (2019). Antecedents of Team Potency and Team Effectiveness: An Examination of Goal and Process Clarity and Servant Leadership. Retrieved from https://www.researchgate.net/publication/ 49834920_Antecedents_of_Team_Potency _and_Team_Effectiveness_An_Examinati on_of_Goal_and_Process_Clarity_and_Se rvant_Leadership

Jenkins, M., & Stewart, A. (2019). The importance of a servant leader orientaton. Retrieved from https://www.researchgate.net/publication/ 40687613_The_importance_of_a_servant _leader_orientaton

Patrnchak, J. (2019). Implementing Servant

Leadership atCleveland Clinic: A Case Study inOrganizational Change. Retrieved from https://csuepress.columbusstate.edu/sltp/vol2/iss1/3/

When bosses 'serve' their employees, everything improves. (2019). Retrieved from https://www.sciencedaily.com/releases/2015/05/150506084804.htm

(2019). Retrieved from https://www.linkedin.com/in/margotmazur/

Harrold, N. (2019). Nikoletta Vecsei Harrold, Author at The Content Wrangler. Retrieved from https://thecontentwrangler.com/author/nikschen/#

HubSpot Blogs | Marketing | Margot Mazur. (2019). Retrieved from https://blog.hubspot.com/marketing/author/margot-mazur

Suzi Nelson. (2019). Retrieved from https://www.crunchbase.com/person/suzi-nelson#section-overview

Made in the USA
Monee, IL
07 October 2022

15403025R00114